D1558906

CITIZEN
HAMILTON

CITIZEN HAMILTON

The Wit and Wisdom of an American Founder

Edited by

DONALD R. HICKEY
AND CONNIE D. CLARK

ROWMAN & LITTLEFIELD PUBLISHERS, INC.
Lanham • Boulder • New York • Toronto • Oxford

ROWMAN & LITTLEFIELD PUBLISHERS, INC.

Published in the United States of America
by Rowman & Littlefield Publishers, Inc.
A wholly owned subsidiary of The Rowman & Littlefield Publishing
Group, Inc.
4501 Forbes Boulevard, Suite 200, Lanham, Maryland 20706
www.rowmanlittlefield.com

PO Box 317
Oxford
OX2 9RU, UK

Distributed by National Book Network

British Library Cataloguing in Publication Information Available

Library of Congress Cataloging-in-Publication Data

Hamilton, Alexander, 1757–1804.
  [Selections. 2005]
  Citizen Hamilton : the wit and wisdom of an American founder /
edited by Donald R. Hickey and Connie D. Clark.
      p. cm.
  Includes bibliographical references and index.
  ISBN 0-7425-4975-5 (cloth : alk. paper)
  1. Hamilton, Alexander, 1757–1804—Quotations. 2. United States—
Politics and government—1775–1783—Quotations, maxims, etc. 3.
United States—Politics and government—1783–1809—Quotations,
maxims, etc. I. Hickey, Donald R., 1944– II. Clark, Connie D., 1957–
III. Title.
  E302.H22 2005
  973.4'092—dc22

                                                2005012520

Printed in the United States of America

♾™ The paper used in this publication meets the minimum
requirements of American National Standard for Information
Sciences—Permanence of Paper for Printed Library Materials,
ANSI/NISO Z39.48-1992.

For our parents:
Jerry Clark
and in memory of
Donna Clark and John and Louise Hickey

Behold Columbia's empire rise,
On freedom's solid base to stand;
Supported by propitious skies,
And seal'd by her deliverer's hand.

Chorus

Raise, Columbia, raise thy voice,
Union is thy noble choice.

.   .   .

The hero, statesman and the sage,
Matur'd this noblest work of man;
And HAMILTON'S instructive page
Illumes his fellow-patriot's plan.

Chorus

Raise, Columbia, raise thy voice,
Union is thy noble choice.

—Albany *Journal*, August 4, 1788

CONTENTS

INTRODUCTION

A man of extraordinary talent and boundless energy, Alexander Hamilton left a remarkable legacy as a soldier, statesman, financier, and lawyer. Although he is usually remembered as an impetuous man of action, the written word played a central role in his life. It enabled him to escape poverty and a humdrum life in the West Indies; it helped him make a name for himself as an opponent of British imperial policy in the Thirteen Colonies; it played a central role in his service as George Washington's most trusted staff officer during the American Revolution; and it was a crucial tool for promoting the policies that he favored in the formative years of the United States. Hamilton used the written word to good effect, but his unrestrained candor coupled with a refusal to disavow unpopular opinions made him many enemies. Among admirers and detractors alike, Hamilton will always be remembered not only for what he did but also for what he wrote.

Hamilton was born on the British island of Nevis in the Caribbean in 1755 or 1757. Although Hamilton preferred that later date, a contemporary court record suggests that the earlier one is correct. Hamilton's parents never married, and John Adams's characterization of him as "the bastard brat of a Scottish peddler" was vicious but technically correct. Hamilton's ne'er-do-well father abandoned the family when he was only ten, and when his mother died three years later, Hamilton found himself virtually an orphan on the Danish island of St. Croix.

1

Bright, hard-working, and ambitious, Hamilton showed such promise that several older men on St. Croix looked after him. The Rev. Hugh Knox saw to Hamilton's education, and Nicolas Cruger, who had the largest trading house on St. Croix, gave Hamilton a position as a clerk in his firm. Hamilton learned a great deal from these men, and the foundation he built under their tutelage served him well in later life.

In 1772 Hamilton wrote a letter describing a hurricane that struck St. Croix. The publication of this stirring letter convinced his friends to send him to the American mainland for further education. Hamilton spent a year at a preparatory school in New Jersey and then, characteristically, refused to enroll in the College of New Jersey (now Princeton University) because its president would not allow him to tackle the program of study at an accelerated pace. Hamilton enrolled instead in King's College (now Columbia University) in New York City. By this time he had developed the lifelong habit of reading voraciously.

At King's College, Hamilton applied himself assiduously to his studies, but was soon drawn into the growing controversy between Great Britain and the Thirteen Colonies. Upholding the Patriot cause, he made his public debut in the summer of 1774 with a rousing speech at a popular meeting. He followed with a pair of lengthy pamphlets—*A Full Vindication of the Measures of Congress* and *The Farmer Refuted*—that challenged British colonial policies. These pamphlets combined stinging invective with such learned arguments that they appeared to be the work of a more mature writer.

After the cold war with the mother country erupted into a shooting war at Lexington and Concord in April of 1775, Hamilton set about organizing an artillery company. Commissioned a captain in the New York Line, he took part in the campaigns in the Middle States. The talent that he showed for organization and leadership and the energy and courage that he displayed in battle won for him a growing reputation. In early 1777 George Washington, who was commander in chief of the Continental Army, invited Hamilton to join his staff as an aide-de-camp with the rank of lieutenant colonel. For a young man of twenty-two, this was an exceptional opportunity, and Hamilton put his talent for writing to good use, drafting orders and composing letters for the commander in chief. Such was Washington's growing confidence in his young aide that he relied increasingly on him for military advice, gave him difficult and delicate diplomatic assignments, and dispatched him on dangerous but indispensable scouting missions. When France entered the war as an ally of the United States in 1778, Hamilton's fluency in French made him even more valuable to Washington.

"The Little Lion," as Hamilton was now called, became Washington's favorite subordinate, serving as a substitute son for the childless Washington, just as Washington was a kind of surrogate father for Hamilton. Nevertheless, Hamilton chafed at his dependence on Washington and longed for an opportunity to win military honor and glory on the battlefield. Accordingly, in early 1781, he used a petty quarrel as an excuse to resign from Washington's staff so that he might return to the field. Securing a command at the siege of Yorktown, he took part in the last great military operation of the American Revolution.

In the 1780s, Hamilton again put his talent for writing to work. To prepare for the New York bar, he wrote a Practice Manual that was widely copied and later served as the basis for a published guide. He also wrote letters and newspaper articles urging that the Articles of Confederation, the nation's first constitution, be amended to grant the feeble central government more power, particularly the power to impose taxes. Since no amendment could be adopted without the approval of all thirteen states, Hamilton's efforts were in vain. In 1786 Hamilton attended the Annapolis Convention, where he proposed a convention of all the states to revise the Articles of Confederation. This was the genesis of the Philadelphia Constitutional Convention that met in the summer of 1787.

As one of the New York delegates, Hamilton spoke sparingly at the Constitutional Convention. What he did say in a 5-hour address delivered on June 18 indicated that he favored a far stronger central government than his fellow delegates. "The gentleman from New York," said Connecticut delegate William S. Johnson, "is praised by every gentleman, but supported by no gentleman." The document that emerged from Philadelphia that summer was a far cry from Hamilton's vision. Nevertheless, he was convinced that the new Constitution was such a dramatic improvement over the old Arti-cles of Confederation that he worked tirelessly for its ratification.

To promote support and understanding for the new Constitution, Hamilton joined James Madison and John Jay in producing *The Federalist*, a series of essays that closely examined the new compact. Hamilton wrote at least 52 of the 85 essays, which are now considered the greatest commentary ever written on the Constitution. Hamilton also attended New York's ratifying convention in Poughkeepsie, where he spoke frequently and effectively, helping to turn a large and hostile majority around on the issue of ratification.

Once the Constitution had been ratified, the first national elections were held, and in the spring of 1789 the new government was launched. Several months later, Congress authorized the creation of executive departments, and President Washington invited Hamilton to join his cabinet as the first secretary of the treasury. With the nation's finances in a deplorable state, this was widely considered to be the most important position in the cabinet. Hamilton eagerly accepted the assignment and threw himself into his new job.

In a series of lengthy and now legendary reports presented to Congress in the early 1790s, Hamilton called for overhauling the nation's finances. He insisted that the new government assume responsibility not only for the debts that it had incurred during the American Revolution but also for those run up by the states. The face value of these two classes of debts was $74 million. This entire sum, Hamilton argued, must be paid at full face value, 100 cents on the dollar, even though much of the indebtedness had been incurred at inflated wartime prices. To repudiate any portion of this debt, Hamilton believed, would undermine the credit worthiness of the government and make it difficult if not impossible to borrow money in future crises.

Hamilton also called for a series of internal or excise taxes to go along with the external taxes on shipping and trade that Congress had adopted before he took office. Hamilton favored the internal taxes both to provide an alternative source of revenue to the taxes on trade and to distribute a portion of the nation's tax burden to the interior, where few imported goods were consumed.

Finally, Hamilton called for the creation of a national bank. Such an institution, he argued, was necessary to provide the government with a safe depository for its funds and a convenient source for short-term loans. In addition, the notes issued by the national bank were expected to serve as a kind of national currency, at least in the larger cities. When the emerging Republican party under Thomas Jefferson and James Madison challenged the constitutionality of the bank, Hamilton, working at breakneck speed, wrote a compelling 15,000-word response that upheld the bank's constitutionality by developing the doctrine of implied powers.

Congress enacted most of Hamilton's financial proposals into law, and the result was a stunning turnaround in the nation's public finances. Almost singlehandedly, Hamilton had created the budget, tax, debt, and national banking system that has been at the heart of American public finance ever since and that is still the envy of the world. For this accomplishment, Hamilton is justly regarded as the greatest secretary of the treasury in the history of the Republic and perhaps the greatest financier who ever lived.

As a member of Washington's cabinet, Hamilton also worked to implement other programs to make the fledgling Republic more secure. He favored a program of military preparedness, both to deter war and to enable the nation to prosecute it more effectively. He also promoted peace and expanded trade with Great Britain, a policy that was cemented in 1795 when President Washington (with Senate approval) ratified the treaty that John Jay had negotiated the year before. The Jay Treaty ushered in an era of Anglo-American accord that fostered American trade and economic growth.

During his tenure as secretary of the treasury, Hamilton's output as a writer was prodigious. He issued lengthy reports to Congress, made written recommendations on a host of petitions, corresponded extensively with customs agents and other government officials, and continued to carry on his usual correspondence with friends and acquaintances.

By 1795, Hamilton had served in Washington's cabinet for more than five years, and most of the policies that he favored were now in place. Hence he resigned from office and returned to New York City to practice law. The only blight on what was otherwise the most stellar and productive period in his life was an ill-advised affair with a woman of dubious reputation by the name of Maria Reynolds. Hamilton was later blackmailed by Reynolds and her husband.

After returning to private life in New York City, Hamilton turned his prodigious energy to representing his clients in court. His practice was extensive and wide-ranging. His cases involved constitutional and public law; real estate, commercial, and maritime law; and even criminal law. He was in great demand, and despite a modest fee schedule, he probably had the richest law practice in America.

Such was Hamilton's talent for making compelling legal arguments that many of those who saw him in action considered him the crown jewel of the American bar. The eminent jurist James Kent, who was Hamilton's younger contemporary, described him as "sublimely eloquent." "His pre-eminence [at the bar]," Kent said, "was at once and universally conceded." After seeing Hamilton argue a case, U.S. Supreme Court Justice James Iredell spoke approvingly of his "astonishing ability," and rival lawyer Brockholst Livingston said "that no event in the course of my professional career has ever given me more concern or excited so much astonishment [as] the influence of Mr. Hamilton with the Court."

Hamilton contributed to the development of American constitutional law in two ways. First and most importantly, in his state papers and other writings he articulated certain fundamental principles—such as the notion of judicial review, the doctrine of implied powers, and the idea of the general welfare—that found their way into American constitutional law. Secondly, as a practicing attorney, he made such compelling arguments that his interpretation of the law often prevailed.

In the *Hylton* case in 1796, Hamilton established broad parameters for the federal government's power to tax. That same year, in one of the cases connected to the Yazoo land frauds in Georgia, Hamilton fixed the meaning of the Constitution's contract clause. In *Rutgers v. Waddington* (1784), he argued that any state law that violated national treaties was null and void. Three years later this principle was embodied in the supremacy clause of the Constitution. Similarly, in the *Croswell* case (1804), Hamilton called for discarding English precedents and allowing truth as a defense in seditious libel cases. This idea was incorporated into state law in 1805 and enshrined in the New York state constitution in 1821.

Despite retiring to private life, Hamilton still took a keen interest in public affairs, and he continued to use his pen to promote the policies he favored. He wrote the first draft of Washington's famous Farewell Address in 1796, and he authored numerous letters and pamphlets promoting Federalist causes and attacking his Republican enemies.

Hamilton returned to public life in the late 1790s, when he served as inspector general of the army during the Quasi-War with France. Besides turning loose his energies on the daunting task of organizing the expanded army, Hamilton used the French crisis to promote the Federalist program of military preparedness. In fact, he gave so much advice to the hapless James McHenry that Hamilton himself became the de facto secretary of war.

Hamilton's writings were not always well advised. In one pamphlet, he explained his affair with Maria Reynolds to disprove charges that his payments to the Reynoldses were part of an illegal scheme to defraud the Treasury. In another, he accused President John Adams of mismanaging the nation's foreign policy with France. Although this pamphlet was intended for private circulation, Republicans secured a copy and published excerpts, forcing Hamilton to make the entire work public. This embarrassed the Federalist party during the election of 1800, although it probably was not the cause of Adams's defeat.

When Thomas Jefferson and Aaron Burr, the two Republican candidates in 1800, each received the same number of votes in the electoral college, the election was thrown into the House of Representatives. Once again Hamilton put pen to paper, this time to promote the defeat of Burr, whom Hamilton considered an unprincipled adventurer who posed a much graver danger to the fragile young republic than the more cautious and temporizing Jefferson. Hamilton got his way when

Jefferson won on the 36th ballot, although it is not clear whether his letter-writing campaign had any effect on the outcome.

Three years later, when Burr made a bid to win the governorship of New York, Hamilton again opposed him, and once again Burr was defeated. Convinced that Hamilton had slandered him, Burr challenged his fellow New Yorker to a duel. Although Hamilton opposed dueling on religious and moral grounds and had even lost his eldest son in a duel in 1801, he felt duty-bound to meet Burr on the field of honor. Thus, in the early morning hours of July 11, 1804, the two men and their seconds rowed across the Hudson River to the traditional dueling ground at Weehawken on the Jersey side.

In the ensuing "interview of honor," Hamilton threw his fire away, but Burr took deadly aim, and his musket ball found its mark, piercing Hamilton's liver and lodging in his spine. Thirty painful hours later, Hamilton, only forty-nine years old, met his maker. He died in debt, partly because of the large investments he had made in western lands and partly because of the money he had lavished on the country estate he was building in Harlem.

Hamilton left a remarkable public legacy. No less a figure than Count Talleyrand, who was well-traveled and had connections on both sides of the Atlantic, considered Hamilton the preeminent figure of the age, superior even to Washington and Napoleon. Although his accomplishments were legion, Hamilton's greatest achievements were putting the nation's financial house in order and establishing the environment in which the American economy could flourish.

Although usually portrayed as a conservative, Hamilton had a vision that looked to the future. He was more interested in building a great nation than in conserving any remnant of the past. If he distrusted the masses, it was because he despised demagoguery and mobocracy and believed in the rule of the law. Moreover, he favored universal manhood suffrage and public education, and he took progressive positions on the abolition of slavery, the treatment of Indians, and freedom of speech. An advocate of meritocracy, he was also an early champion of promoting enlisted men into the army's officer corps.

Not only did Hamilton play a central role in shaping the new nation, but even though he never saw his fiftieth birthday, he left a larger body of written material than any other Founder. More than anyone else of his generation, he was blessed with such remarkable energy and was consumed by such a powerful desire to analyze, explain, and persuade that he wrote almost incessantly. Writing at breakneck speed, he sometimes fractured his syntax, and he was often verbose. Nevertheless, his message was always clear. If he lacked the wit or eloquence of a Franklin, Jefferson, or Lincoln, his writing style was nonetheless direct and forceful, and his arguments—usually bottomed on basic principles—were compelling.

It was the Age of the Pamphlet, and in the sheer volume of his output, the erudition that he displayed, and the range of topics that he tackled, Hamilton established himself as one of the leading pamphleteers of his generation. Impressed by his output, Jefferson once characterized Hamilton as "a colossus of the anti-republican party." "Without numbers," the Sage of Monticello concluded, "he is an host within himself." Hamilton's energy and ambition, his need to be understood, and his will to succeed, all still show through in his writings, and many of the messages that he delivered so forcefully more than 200 years ago are still relevant today.

A NOTE ON SOURCES AND EDITORIAL STYLE

Almost all quotations that follow have been taken from the comprehensive 27-volume *Papers of Alexander Hamilton*, edited by Harold C. Syrett and others. A few quotations have also been gleaned from the 5-volume *Law Practice of Alexander Hamilton*, edited by Julius Goebel, Jr., and others. Full citations for both works can be found in the Select Annotated Bibliography that appears at the end of this work. The Syrett collection offers such an abundance of material that we did not consider it necessary to draw upon remarks attributed to Hamilton by his contemporaries, especially since so many of these attributions are dubious.

Although we have left some of Hamilton's writing mannerisms intact, we have generally modernized capitalization and spelling and silently corrected obvious writing errors. In every other way, we have tried to remain true to the original. If we have deleted any material from a quotation, we have so indicated with an ellipse (. . .). Likewise, when we have inserted any explanatory material, we have put it in square brackets [ ].

In the reference that follows each quotation, we have put in italics works published separately as books or pamphlets as well as major reports; essays that appeared in newspapers are set off by quotation marks; and unpublished manuscripts as well as speeches appear in simple roman type.

CHRONOLOGY OF ALEXANDER HAMILTON 1755-1804

1755: (January 11) Born on Nevis in British West Indies

1765: Father abandons family
Family moves to St. Croix in Danish West Indies

1768: Mother dies
Becomes apprentice clerk in firm of Cruger and Beckman

1772: Writes letter describing hurricane
Travels to New Jersey for schooling

1773: Enrolls in King's College in New York City

1774: Delivers speech upholding Patriot cause
Publishes *A Full Vindication of the Measures of Congress* defending Patriot response to British colonial policy

1775: Publishes *The Farmer Refuted* defending American rights

1775–77: Takes part in military campaigns in middle states

1776: Is commissioned a captain in New York Line

1777: Appointed to George Washington's staff at rank of lieutenant colonel
Writes notes in "Pay Book" on a wide range of subjects

1778:	Publishes "Publius Letters" attacking Samuel Chase for trying to corner flour market
1780:	Marries Elizabeth Schuyler
1781:	Resigns from Washington's staff Takes part in Battle of Yorktown
1781-82:	Publishes "The Continentalist" essays calling for stronger Confederation government
1782:	Son Philip is born (seven other children follow) Writes Practice Manual to prepare for bar Admitted to New York bar Admitted to New York Chancery Court
1782–83:	Serves in Confederation Congress
1783:	Becomes member of Society of Cincinnati Prepares Report on a Military Peace Establishment for Confederation Congress Proposes constitutional convention to revise Articles of Confederation Opens law office on Wall Street in New York City
1784:	Publishes *Phocion* letters calling for better treatment of Loyalists Argues in *Rutgers v. Waddington* for supremacy of national treaties Helps establish Bank of New York
1785:	Helps establish New York Society for Promoting the Manumission of Slaves
1786:	Attends Annapolis Convention; proposes convention to revise Articles of Confederation Brother James dies in West Indies
1787:	Serves in New York State Assembly Attends Philadelphia Constitutional Convention
1787–88:	Publishes *The Federalist* papers examining the new Constitution
1788:	Attends New York ratifying convention Serves in Continental Congress

1789:	Publishes "H. G." letters attacking Governor George Clinton of New York
	Appointed Secretary of the Treasury
1790:	Issues first *Report on Public Credit*
	Awarded honorary Doctor of Laws by Dartmouth College
	Issues *Report on a National Bank*
1791:	Issues *Report on the Establishment of a Mint*
	Elected to American Philosophical Society
	Writes Opinion on Constitutionality of an Act to Establish a National Bank, developing doctrine of implied powers
	Helps establish Society for Establishing Useful Manufactures
	Elected to American Academy of Arts and Sciences
	Issues *Report on the Subject of Manufactures*
1791–92:	Has affair with Maria Reynolds
1792:	Writes letter to Edward Carrington of Virginia defending himself against attacks from Jefferson and Madison
	Writes "The Vindication" essays defending funding system
	Publishes "T.L." and "An American" letters attacking Jefferson for employing critic Philip Freneau in government service
	Publishes "Civis" and "Fact" letters defending his handling of national debt
	Awarded honorary Doctor of Laws by Harvard College
	Publishes "Catullus" and "Metellus" essays attacking Jefferson
1792 or 93:	Writes View of the Commercial Regulations of France and Great Britain in Reference to the United States
1793:	Agrees to serve as trustee of Hamilton Oneida Academy (now Hamilton College)

15

Issues reports responding to congressional resolutions of William Branch Giles criticizing his handling of two national loans

Publishes "Pacificus" and "Philo Pacificus" essays defending President Washington's Neutrality Proclamation

Publishes "No Jacobin" essays defending U.S. policy toward France

1794: Orchestrates federal response to Whiskey Rebellion

Publishes "Tully" essays defending suppression of Whiskey Rebellion

1795: Issues Final *Report on Public Credit*

Resigns as secretary of treasury

Resumes law practice in New York City

Writes Remarks on Jay Treaty for President Washington

Writes The Defence of the Funding System

1795–96: Publishes "Camillus" and "Philo-Camillus" essays defending Jay Treaty

1796: Admitted to practice in U.S. Supreme Court

Writes draft of Washington's Farewell Address

1797: Publishes "The Warning" essays attacking France

Publishes *Observations on Certain Documents* explaining affair with Maria Reynolds

1798: Publishes "The Stand" essays attacking France

Appointed Inspector General of Army during Quasi-War with France at the rank of major general

1799: Father dies on St. Vincent in West Indies

1800: Discharged from Army

Publishes *Letter from Alexander Hamilton, Concerning the Public Conduct and Character of John Adams* attacking Adams

1800–1801: Supports Thomas Jefferson over Aaron Burr for presidency

1801:	Publishes *An Address to the Electors of the State of New-York* defending Federalist policies Establishes New York *Evening Post* Son Philip killed in duel
1801–02:	Publishes "The Examination" essays attacking Jefferson and his policies
1802:	Calls for creation of Christian Constitutional Society to promote Federalist causes
1803:	Publishes "Pericles" letter calling for seizure of Louisiana from France Helps establish Merchants' Bank in New York City
1804:	Defends free speech in *People v. Croswell* Opposes Burr's election as governor of New York (July 12) Dies from duel with Burr Buried in Trinity Churchyard in New York City

THE WORDS OF
ALEXANDER HAMILTON

John Adams

❧ ❦

Mr. Adams like other men has his faults and foibles . . . but we believe him to be honest, firm, faithful, and independent; a sincere lover of his country; a real friend to genuine liberty but combining his attachment to that with the love of order and stable government. No man's private character can be fairer than his. No man has given stronger proofs than him of disinterested and intrepid patriotism.

To John Steele, Philadelphia, October 15, 1792

Mr. Adams has governed and must govern from *impulse* and *caprice*, under the influence of the two most mischievous of passions for a politician . . . *Vanity* and *Jealousy*.

To Charles Carroll of Carrollton, New York, August 7, 1800

It is a fact that he is often liable to paroxysms of anger, which deprive him of self command, and produce very outrageous behavior to those who approach him.

Letter from Alexander Hamilton,
Concerning the Public Conduct and
Character of John Adams, New York, October 24, 1800

He has certain fixed points of character which tend naturally to the detriment of any cause of which he is the chief, of any administration of which he is the head; that by his ill humors and jealousies he has already divided and distracted the supporters of the government; that he has furnished deadly weapons to its enemies by unfounded accusations, and has weakened the force of its friends by decrying some of the most influential of them to the utmost of his power.

Letter from Alexander Hamilton,
Concerning the Public Conduct and
Character of John Adams, New York, October 24, 1800

Affection

❧ ❧

We love our families more than our neighbors. We love our neighbors more than our countrymen in general. The human affections, like the solar heat, lose their intensity as they depart from the center, and become languid in proportion to the expansion of the circle on which they act.

Speech at New York Ratifying Convention,
Poughkeepsie, New York, June 27, 1788

Aggression

❧ ❧

Our true policy is, in the attitude of calm defiance, to meet the aggressions upon us by proportionate resistance, and to prepare vigorously for further resistance.

"The Stand No. VI," New York,
April 19, 1798

Agriculture

❧ ❧

It ought readily to be conceded that the cultivation of the earth—as the primary and most certain source of national supply, as the immediate and chief source of subsistence to man, as the principal source of those materials which constitute the nutriment of other kinds of labor, as including a state most favorable to the freedom and independence of the human mind, one, perhaps, most conducive to the multiplication of the human species—has intrinsically a strong claim to pre-eminence over every other kind of industry.

Report on the Subject of Manufactures,
Philadelphia, December 5, 1791

That among the objects of labor and industry, agriculture considered with reference either to individual or national welfare is first in importance may safely be affirmed without derogating from the just and real value of any other branch. It is indeed the best basis of the prosperity of every other.

Draft of George Washington's Eighth
Annual Address to Congress,
New York, November 10, 1796

Agriculture and Commerce

❧

Nothing can be more mistaken than the collision and rivalship which almost always subsist between the landed and trading interests, for the truth is they are so inseparably interwoven that one cannot be injured without injury, nor benefitted without benefit to the other. Oppress trade, lands sink in value; make it flourish, their value rises; encumber husbandry, trade declines; encourage agriculture, commerce revives.

"The Continentalist No. VI," Fishkill,
New York, July 4, 1782

Their interests are intimately blended and interwoven.

The Federalist No. 12, New York,
November 27, 1787

Aide-de-Camp

❧ ❧

I always disliked the office of an Aide-de-Camp as having in it a kind of personal dependence.

To Philip Schuyler, Windsor,
New York, February 18, 1781

Alcohol

❧ ❧

The consumption of ardent spirits particularly, no doubt very much on account of their cheapness, is carried to an extreme, which is truly to be regretted, as well in regard to the health and the morals, as to the economy of the community.

Report on Public Credit,
New York, January 9, 1790

Allies

❧ ❧

The ally of our ally has no claim, as such, to our friendship.

To George Washington, New York,
September 15, 1790

Ambition

My ambition is prevalent [so] that I contemn the groveling and condition of a clerk or the like, to which my fortune etc. condemns me and would willingly risk my life, though not my character, to exalt my station. . . . I wish there was a war.

To Edward Stevens, St. Croix, November 11, 1769

Great ambition unchecked by principle, or the love of glory, is an unruly tyrant which never can keep long in a course which good men will approve.

To James A. Bayard, New York, January 16, 1801

American Character

There is a total dissimulation in the circumstances, as well as the manners, of society among us; and it is as ridiculous to seek for models in the simple ages of Greece and Rome as it would be to go in quest of them among the Hottentots and Laplanders.

"The Continentalist No. VI," Fishkill, New York, July 4, 1782

The people of the United States are a people equally sober and enlightened; their notions of liberty are rational and orderly.

"No Jacobin No. VIII," Philadelphia, August 26, 1793

Our Country is not a military one.

To William Loughton Smith, New York, April 10, 1797

Self-sufficiency and a contempt of the science and experience of others are too prevailing traits of character in this country.

To John Jay, Philadelphia, November 19, 1798

The American Revolution

❧ ☙

Our affairs are in a bad way; but I hope they will end well. Europe will save us in spite of ourselves.

To John Laurens, Middle Brook,
New Jersey, May 22, 1779

Anarchy

❧ ☙

A large and well organized Republic can scarcely lose its liberty from any other cause than that of anarchy, to which a contempt of the laws is the high road.

"Tully No. III," Philadelphia, August 28, 1794

Ancestry

❧ ☙

The truth is that on the question of who my parents were, I have better pretensions than most of those who in this country plume themselves on ancestry.

To William Jackson, New York, August 26, 1800

Argumentation

❧ ❧

To overrate the value or force of our own arguments is a natural foible of self love—to be convinced without convincing others is no uncommon fate of a writer or speaker.

"The Defence No. XXII," New York, November 5-11, 1795

The Army

❧ ❧

I religiously believe the officers of the army are among the best citizens in America and inviolably attached to the liberties of the community, infinitely more so than any of those splenetic patriots out of it who endeavor for sinister purposes to instill jealousies and alarms which they themselves know to be as groundless as they are impolitic and ridiculous.

To William Gordon, West Point, September 5, 1779

The entire formation and disposal of our military forces ought to belong to Congress. It is an essential cement of the union; and it ought to be the policy of Congress to des[troy] all ideas of state attachments in the army and make it look up wholly to them.

To James Duane, Liberty Pole, New Jersey, September 3, 1780

The licentiousness of an army is to be dreaded in every government; but in a republic it is more particularly to be restrained, and when directed against the civil authority to be checked with energy and punished with severity.

To John Dickinson, Albany, New York,
September 25-30, 1783

Army Chaplains

He is just what I should like for a military parson except that he does not whore or drink. He will fight, and he will not insist upon your going to heaven whether you will or not.

To Anthony Wayne, Preakness,
New Jersey, July 6, 1780

The Articles of Confederation

We have now happily concluded the great work of independence, but much remains to be done to reach the fruits of it. Our prospects are not flattering. Every day proves the inefficacy of the present confederation; yet the common danger being removed, we are receding instead of advancing in a disposition to amend its defects.

To John Jay, Philadelphia,
July 25, 1783

Avarice

When avarice takes the lead in a state, it is commonly the forerunner of its fall.

"Publius Letter, I," Poughkeepsie,
New York, October 16, 1778

Bad Men

❧ ❧

Bad men are apt to paint others like themselves.

A Full Vindication of the Measures of Congress,
New York, December 15, 1774

Banks

❧ ❧

Banks are essential to the pecuniary operations of the government.

Report on the State of the Treasury, Philadelphia, February 19,
1793

Blacks

❧ ❧

I have not the least doubt that the negroes will make very excellent soldiers with the proper management.

To John Jay, Middlebrook, New Jersey, March 14, 1779

I frequently hear it objected to the scheme of embodying negroes that they are too stupid to make soldiers. This is so far from appearing to me a valid objection that I think their want of cultivation (for their natural faculties are probably as good as ours) joined to that habit of subordination which they acquire from a life of servitude will make them sooner become soldiers than our White inhabitants.

To John Jay, Middlebrook, New Jersey, March 14, 1779

I foresee that this project [to employ southern slaves in the Revolutionary War] will have to combat much opposition from prejudice and self-interest. The contempt we have been taught to entertain for the blacks, makes us fancy many things that are founded neither in reason nor experience; and an unwillingness to part with property of so valuable a kind will furnish a thousand arguments to show the impracticability or pernicious tendency of a scheme which requires such a sacrifice. But it should be considered that if we do not make use of them in this way, the enemy probably will; and that the best way to counteract the temptations they will hold out will be to offer them ourselves. An essential part of the plan is to give them their freedom with their muskets. This will secure their fidelity, animate their courage, and I believe will have a good influence upon those who remain by opening a door to their emancipation. This circumstance, I confess, has no small weight in inducing me to wish the success of the project; for the dictates of humanity and true policy equally interest me in favor of this unfortunate class of men.

To John Jay, Middlebrook, New Jersey, March 14, 1779

Brevity

In all military documents it is peculiarly desirable to consult conciseness as far as it may comport with perspicuity and accuracy. Military men in the midst of active operations have very little leisure for writing.

To Caleb Swan, New York,
September 22, 1799

Aaron Burr

※ ※

If we have an embryo-Caesar in the United States, 'tis Burr.

> To —, Philadelphia, September 26, 1792

[If elected President] Burr will certainly attempt to reform the government *a la Buonaparte*. He is as unprincipled and dangerous a man as any country can boast; as true a *Cataline* as ever met in midnight conclave.

> To James A. Bayard, New York, August 6, 1800

As to *Burr*, there is nothing in his favor. His private character is not defended by his most partial friends. He is bankrupt beyond redemption except by the plunder of his country. His public principles have no other spring or aim than his own aggrandizement per *fas* et *nefas [justly or unjustly]*.

> To Oliver Wolcott, Jr., New York,
> December 16, 1800

Burr loves nothing but himself, thinks of nothing but his own aggrandizement, and will be content with nothing short of permanent power in his own hands.

> To Harrison Gray Otis, New York,
> December 23, 1800

He is far more *cunning* than *wise*, far more *dexterous* than *able*.

> To James A. Bayard, New York,
> January 16, 1801

The Canadian-American Border

It may be desired and would it not be our interest to agree that neither party shall in time of peace keep up any armed force upon the lakes nor any fortified places nearer than miles to the lakes except small posts for small guards (the number to be defined) stationed for the security of trading houses?

Memorandum on Instructions for John Jay,
Philadelphia, April 23, 1794

Candor

I thought it my duty to exhibit things as they are, not as they ought to be.

To Robert Morris, Albany, New York, August 13, 1782

Capital Punishment

The temper of our country is not a little opposed to the frequency of capital punishment. Public opinion in this respect, though it must not have too much influence, is not wholly to be disregarded.

To James McHenry, New York, July 29, 1799

Character

❦

I am aware that a man of real merit is never seen in so favorable a light as through the medium of adversity. The clouds that surround him are shades that set off his good qualities. Misfortune cuts down the little vanities that in prosperous times served as so many spots in his virtues and gives a tone of humility that makes his worth more amiable.

To John Laurens, Preakness, New Jersey, October 11, 1780

Christian Fortitude

❦

We live in a world full of evil. In the later period of life misfortunes seem to thicken round us; and our duty and our peace both require that we should accustom ourselves to meet disasters with Christian fortitude.

To Elizabeth Hamilton, New York, March 16-17, 1803

Civil Disobedience

❦

The theory of every constitution presupposes as a *first principle* that the *laws are to be obeyed*. There can therefore be no such thing as a "constitutional resistance" to laws constitutionally enacted.

To George Washington, Philadelphia, September 2, 1794

Civil War

❧ ☙

Civil war is undoubtedly a great evil. It is one that every good man would wish to avoid and will deplore if inevitable. But it is incomparably a less evil than the destruction of government.

"Tully No. IV," Philadelphia, September 2, 1794

Coercion

❧ ☙

'Tis only to consult our own hearts to be convinced that nations like individuals revolt at the idea of being guided by external compulsion. They will at least only yield to that idea after resistance has been fruitlessly tried in all its forms.

To George Washington, Philadelphia, April 14, 1794

Colonialism

❧ ☙

His Holiness the Pope, by virtue of being Christ's Vicegerent upon earth, piously assumed to himself a right to dispose of the territories of infidels as he thought fit. And in process of time, all Christian princes learned to imitate his example, very liberally giving and granting away the dominion and property of pagan countries. They did not seem to be satisfied with the title which Christianity gave them to the next world only; but chose to infer from thence an exclusive right to this world also.

The Farmer Refuted, New York,
February 23, 1775

Committees

There is always more decision, more dispatch, more secrecy, more responsibility where single men, than [where] bodies are concerned.

To Anthony Wayne, Morristown,
New Jersey, December 28, 1779

I proceed to lay it down as a rule that one man of discernment is better fitted to analyze and estimate the peculiar qualities adapted to particular offices than a body of men of equal, or perhaps even of superior, discernment.

The Federalist No. 76, New York,
April 1, 1788

Confessions

'Tis probable, when men are in a confessing mood, that more has been confessed than is true.

To Thomas Willing, Philadelphia,
July 27, 1792

Conformity

Men are fond of going with the stream.

To James Wilson, New York, January 25, 1789

The Constitution

❧ ❧

In reading many of the publications against the Constitution, a man is apt to imagine that he is perusing some ill written tale or romance; which instead of natural and agreeable images exhibits to the mind nothing but frightful and distorted shapes—Gorgons, Hydras, and Chimeras dire—discoloring and disfiguring whatever it represents and transforming every thing it touches into a monster.

The Federalist No. 29, New York,
January 9, 1788

At this moment a most dangerous combination exists. . . . The language in the confidential circles is that the Constitution of the United States is too complex a system—that it savors too much of the pernicious doctrine of "balances and checks," that it requires to be simplified in its structure, to be purged of some monarchical and aristocratic ingredients which are said to have found their way into it, and to be stripped of some dangerous prerogatives with which it is pretended to be invested.

Defense of the President's Neutrality Proclamation,
Philadelphia, May 1793

The abstract idea of regard for a constitution on paper will not long resist a thorough detestation of its practice.

Defense of the President's Neutrality Proclamation,
Philadelphia, May 1793

If it were to be asked, What is the most sacred duty and the greatest source of security in a Republic? The answer would be, an inviolable respect for the Constitution and laws—the first growing out of the last.

"Tully No. III," Philadelphia, August 28, 1794

It is nevertheless too much a fashion with some politicians, when hard pressed on the expediency of a measure, to entrench themselves behind objections to its constitutionality.

"The Defence No. XXXVI," New York,
January 2, 1796

In my opinion the present Constitution is the standard to which we are to cling. Under its banners, *bona fide* must we combat our political foes—rejecting all changes but through the channel itself [that] provides for amendments.

To James A. Bayard, New York,
April 16-21, 1802

Constitutional Law

A sacred respect for the constitutional law is the vital principle, the sustaining energy, of a free government.

"Tully No. III," Philadelphia,
August 28, 1794

Constitutions

Constitutions should consist only of general provisions. The reason is that they must necessarily be permanent and that they cannot calculate for the possible changes of things.

Speech at New York Ratifying Convention,
Poughkeepsie, New York, June 28, 1788

Consumption

❧

I do think we are, and shall be, great consumers.

Conversation with George Beckwith,
New York, October 1789

Continental Congress

❧

Folly, caprice, [and] a want of foresight, comprehension, and dignity characterize the general tenor of [its] actions.

To George Clinton, Valley Forge,
Pennsylvania, February 13, 1778

Contracts

❧

States, like individuals, who observe their engagements are respected and trusted; while the reverse is the fate of those who pursue an opposite conduct.

Report on Public Credit, New York,
January 9, 1790

The Constitution of the United states interdicts the states individually from passing any law impairing the obligation of contracts. This, to the more enlightened part of the community, was not one of the least recommendations of that Constitution.

To George Washington, Philadelphia, May 28, 1790

Controlling Events

❧ ❧

The best way is ever not to attempt to stem a torrent but to divert it.

To George Washington, Philadelphia,
March 17, 1783

Thomas Conway

❧ ❧

He is one of the vermin bred in the entrails of this chimera dire, and there does not exist a more villainous calumniator and incendiary.

To George Clinton, Valley Forge,
Pennsylvania, February 13, 1778

Courts

❧ ❧

There must be an end of all liberty where the Prince is possessed of such exorbitant prerogative as enables him, at pleasure, to establish the most iniquitous, cruel, and oppressive courts of criminal, civil, and ecclesiastical jurisdiction; and to appoint temporary judges and officers whom he can displace and change as often as he pleases.

"Remarks on the Quebec Bill, Part One,"
New York, June 15, 1775

Credit

❧

'Tis in vain to attempt to disparage credit by objecting to its abuses. What is there not liable to abuse or misuse?

Report on Public Credit, Philadelphia,
January 16, 1795

Creditors

❧

Charity itself cannot avoid concluding from the language and conduct of some men (and some of them of no inconsiderable importance) that in their vocabularies *creditor* and *enemy* are synonymous terms and that they have a laudable antipathy against every man to who they owe money either as individuals or as members of the society.

"The Vindication No. II" (second version),
Philadelphia, May-August 1792

Criminal Intent

❧

It may as a general and universal rule be asserted that the intention is never excluded in the consideration of the crime.

Speech in *People v. Croswell*, Albany, New York,
February 14-15, 1804

Crowds

A crowd will always draw a crowd, whatever be the purpose.

To —, Philadelphia, May 18, 1793

Danger

In popular governments 'tis useful that those who propose measures should partake in whatever dangers they may involve.

To Angelica Church, Bedford, Pennsylvania, October 23, 1794

Death

I am disgusted with everything in this world . . . and I have no other wish than as soon as possible to make a brilliant exit. 'Tis a weakness, but I feel I am not fit for this terrestrial country.

To John Laurens, Morristown, New Jersey,
January 8, 1780

This letter, my very dear Eliza, will not be delivered to you, unless I shall first have terminated my earthly career; to begin, as I humbly hope, from redeeming grace and divine mercy a happy immortality.

To Elizabeth Hamilton, New York, July 4, 1804

Debate

❧

In the field of literary contention, it is common to see the epithets *artifice*, *sophistry*, *misrepresentation*, and *abuse* mutually bandied about.

The Farmer Refuted, New York, February 23, 1775

The jinglers who endeavor to cheat us with the sound have never dared to venture into the fair field of argument. They are conscious that it is easier to declaim than to reason on the subject. They know it to be better to play a game with the passions and prejudices than to engage seriously with the understanding of the auditory.

"Tully No. IV," Philadelphia, September 2, 1794

Debts

❧

In the code of moral and political obligations, that of paying debts holds a prominent place.

The Defence of the Funding System, New York, July 1795

Demagogues

❧

Demagogues are not always *inconsiderable* persons. Patricians were frequently demagogues.

Speech at Constitutional Convention,
Philadelphia, June 18, 1787

There is no stronger sign of combinations unfriendly to the general good than when the partisans of those in power raise an indiscriminate cry against men of property.

> "To the Electors of the State of New York,"
> New York, April 7, 1789

It is only to consult the history of nations to perceive that every country at all times is cursed by the existence of men who, actuated by an irregular ambition, scruple [at] nothing which they imagine will contribute to their own advancement and importance. In monarchies [it is] supple courtiers, in republics fawning or turbulent demagogues, worshiping still the idol power wherever placed, whether in the hands of a prince or of the people and trafficking in the weaknesses, vices, frailties, or prejudices of the one or the other.

> "The Defence No. I," New York, July 22, 1795

Democracy

Dismemberment of our Empire will be a clear sacrifice of great positive advantages without any counterbalancing good; administering no relief to our real disease, which is DEMOCRACY.

> To Theodore Sedgwick, New York, July 10, 1804

Depression

I am under a necessity of playing the game of good spirits, but separated from those I love, it is a most artificial game, and at the bottom of my soul there is a more than usual gloom.

> To Elizabeth Hamilton, New Jersey, May 24, 1800

Desertion

❦ ❧

Every day brings fresh proof of the necessity of severe examples to check a wanton spirit of desertion, which if not checked will render the enlistments of soldiers a mere waste of the public treasure.

To James McHenry, New York, July 3, 1799

The proper mode of treating the crime of desertion has been in most countries an embarrassing subject. In ours it is particularly so. The punishment of death except in time of war is contrary to the popular habits of thinking. Whipping is found ineffectual.

To James McHenry, Philadelphia, December 1799

Despotism

❦ ❧

A dangerous ambition more often lurks behind the specious mask of zeal for the rights of the people than under the forbidding appearance of zeal for the firmness and efficiency of government. History will teach us that the former has been found a much more certain road to the introduction of despotism than the latter, and that of those men who have overturned the liberties of republics, the greatest number have begun their career by paying an obsequious court to the people, commencing demagogues and ending tyrants.

The Federalist No. 1, New York, October 27, 1787

Who will have the folly to deny that the definition of despotism is the concentration of all the powers of government in one person or in one body?

"The Examination Number XIV,"
New York, March 2, 1802

Destiny

Mine is an odd destiny. Perhaps no man in the Ustates has sacrificed or done more for the present Constitution than myself, and contrary to all my anticipations of its fate, as you know from the very beginning, I am still laboring to prop the frail and worthless fabric. Yet I have the murmurs of its friends no less than the curses of its foes for my rewards. What can I do better than withdraw from the scene? Every day proves to me more and more that this American world was not made for me.

To Gouverneur Morris, New York, February 29, 1802

Diplomacy

Energy without asperity seems best to comport with the dignity of national language. The force ought to be more in the idea than in the expression or manner.

To Edmund Randolph, Philadelphia, April 27, 1794

Real firmness is good for every thing. *Strut* is good for nothing.

To Oliver Wolcott, Jr., New York, June 6, 1797

Directness

Upon this as upon every other occasion, my desire is to encounter directly and without detour whatever embarrassment may stand in my way.

To George Washington, Philadelphia, April 8, 1794

Discontentment

※ ※

I hate Congress—I hate the army—I hate the world—I hate myself. The whole is a mass of fools and knaves.

To John Laurens, New Bridge, New Jersey,
September 12, 1780

Discrediting Something

※ ※

Neglects and *slights* calculated to lessen the opinion of the importance of a thing and bring it into discredit are often the most successful weapons by which it can be attacked.

"H. G. Letter XII," New York,
March 8, 1789

Discretion

※ ※

A prudent silence will frequently be taken for wisdom, and a sentence or two cautiously thrown in will sometimes gain the palm of knowledge, while a man well informed but indiscreet and unreserved will not uncommonly talk himself out of all consideration and weight.

To James A. Hamilton, New York, June 1804

Discretion is the MENTOR which ought to accompany every Young *Telemachus* in his journey through life.

To James A. Hamilton, New York, June 1804

Divide and Conquer

❧ ❧

Divide et impera [divide and command] must be the motto of every nation that either hates or fears us.

The Federalist No. 7, New York,
November 17, 1787

Division of Labor

❧ ❧

It has justly been observed that there is scarcely anything of greater moment in the economy of a nation than the proper division of labor.

Report on the Subject of Manufactures,
Philadelphia, December 5, 1791

Doing Right

❧ ❧

The real failure to do right . . . often sinks the governments as well as individuals into merited contempt.

The Defence of the Funding System,
New York, July 1795

Let us be *Right*, because to do right is intrinsically proper and I verily believe it is the best means of securing final success.

To Rufus King, New York, April 15, 1796

Dueling

My religious and moral principles are strongly opposed to the practice of dueling, and it would even give me pain to be obliged to shed the blood of a fellow creature in a private combat forbidden by the laws.

> Statement on Impending Duel with Aaron Burr,
> New York, June 28-July 10, 1804

Due Process

I hold it to be a maxim which ought to be sacred in our form of government that no man ought to be deprived of any right or privilege which he enjoys under the Constitution but for some offence proved in due course of law.

> Speech in New York Assembly,
> New York, January 27, 1787

Duty

'Tis a good old maxim to which we may safely adhere in most cases that we ought to do our duty and leave the rest to the care of heaven.

> To William Gordon, West Point,
> New York, September 5, 1779

Do you imagine that any menaces of appeal to the people can induce me to depart from what I conceive to be my public duty!

To Andrew G. Fraunces, Philadelphia,
August 2, 1793

Economic Warfare

❧

I feel a particular reluctance to hazard anything in the present state of our affairs which may lead to commercial warfare with any power, which as far as my knowledge of examples extends is commonly productive of mutual inconvenience and injury and of dispositions tending to a worse kind of warfare.

To Thomas Jefferson, Philadelphia,
January 13, 1791

Efficiency

❧

I cannot make everybody else as rapid as myself.

To Elizabeth Hamilton, Philadelphia,
December 10, 1798

Nothing is more easy than to reduce the number of agents employed in any business and yet for the business to go on with the reduced number. But before the reduction is applauded, it ought to be ascertained that the business is as well done as it was before. There is a wide difference between merely getting along with business and doing it well and effectually.

"The Examination Number X,"
New York, January 19, 1802

Emergencies

In emergencies great and difficult, not to act with an energy proportioned to their magnitude and pressure is as dangerous as any other conceivable course.

> Edmund Randolph to Thomas Mifflin,
> Philadelphia, August 7, 1794

Emotions

Vanity and jealousy exclude all counsel. Passion wrests the helm from reason.

> To Rufus King, New York, January 5, 1800

Enemies

There is no greater error than that of undervaluing an enemy, but with one exception, which is that of overvaluing them.

> To Robert R. Livingston, German Town,
> Pennsylvania, August 7, 1777

In common life, it is readily understood that whoever knowingly assists my enemy to injure me becomes himself, by doing so, my enemy also; and the reason being the same, the rule cannot be different between nations.

> "No Jacobin No. IV," Philadelphia,
> August 10, 1793

No man is without his personal enemies. Pre-eminence even in talents and virtue is a cause of envy and hatred of its possessor. Bad men are the natural enemies of virtuous men. Good men sometimes mistake and dislike each other.

"The Defence No. I," New York, July 22, 1795

Europe

The world may politically as well as geographically be divided into four parts, each having a distinct set of interests. Unhappily for the other three, Europe, by her arms and by her negotiations, by force and by fraud, has in different degrees extended her dominion over them all. Africa, Asia, and America have successively felt her domination. The superiority she has long maintained has tempted her to plume herself as the Mistress of the World, and to consider the rest of mankind as created for her benefit.

The Federalist No. 11, New York, November 24, 1787

A cloud has been for some time hanging over the European world. If it should break forth into a storm, who can insure us that in its progress a part of its fury would not be spent upon us? No reasonable man would hastily pronounce that we are entirely out of its reach.

The Federalist No. 34, New York, January 5, 1788

[Most of Europe] will see in us a people who have a due respect for property and personal security, who in the midst of our revolution abstained with exemplary moderation from every thing violent or sanguinary, instituting governments adequate to the protection of persons and property; who since the completion of our revolution have in a very short period, from mere reasoning and reflection, without tumult or bloodshed, adopted a form of general government calculated as well as the nature of things would permit to remedy antecedent defects, to give strength and security to the Nation, to rest the foundations of liberty on the basis of justice, order, and law—who at all times have been content to govern ourselves; unmeddling in the governments or affairs of other nations.

"Americanus No. II," Philadelphia, February 7, 1794

Factionalism

❧ ❧

That the spirit of faction is a common and one of the most fatal diseases of republics, one which has most frequently wrought their destruction, is a truth witnessed by all history and by all experience.

On James Blanchard, Philadelphia, January 1793

Facts

❧ ❧

Facts . . . speak louder than words, and under certain circumstances louder even than oaths.

"An American No. II," Philadelphia, August 11, 1792

Faults

❧ ❧

There may often be good reasons for *overlooking* a fault which we *perceive*. To *overlook* is very different from *not to see* or not to attend to.

To James McHenry, New York, August 5, 1799

The Federal Government

The Federal Government should neither be independent nor too much dependent. It should neither be raised above responsibility or control, nor should it want the means of maintaining its own weight, authority, dignity, and credit.

"The Continentalist No. VI," Fishkill,
New York, July 4, 1782

Federalism

States will prefer their particular concerns to the general welfare; and as the states become large and important, will they not be less attentive to the general government?

Speech at Constitutional Convention,
Philadelphia, June 18, 1787

It will always be far more easy for the state governments to encroach upon the national authorities than for the national government to encroach upon the state authorities.

The Federalist No. 17, New York, December 5, 1787

Power being almost always the rival of power, the general government will at all times stand ready to check the usurpations of the state governments; and these will have the same disposition towards the general government. The people, by throwing themselves into either scale, will infallibly make it preponderate. If their rights are invaded by either, they can make use of the other as the instrument of redress.

The Federalist No. 28, New York,
December 26, 1787

As to the destruction of state governments, the *great* and *real* anxiety is to be able to preserve the national [government] from the too potent and counteracting influence of those governments.

> To Edward Carrington,
> Philadelphia, May 26, 1792

The theory of our Constitution with respect to taxation is perhaps a new example in the world, that is to say, a concurrent and coordinate authority in one general head and in thirteen (now fifteen) distinct members of a confederacy.

> The Defence of the Funding System,
> New York, July 1795

The Federal Judiciary

It is not only the weakest of the three departments of power, but also, as it regards the security and preservation of civil liberty, by far the safest.

> "The Examination Number XIV,"
> New York, March 2, 1802

Finding a Husband

Get a man of sense, not ugly enough to be pointed at, with some good-nature, a few grains of feeling, a little taste, a little imagination, and above all a good deal of decision to keep you in order, for that I foresee will be no easy task. If you can find one with all these qualities willing to marry you, marry him as soon as you please.

To Margarita Schuyler, New Windsor,
New York, January 21, 1781

Finding a Wife

❦ ❧

She must be young, handsome (I lay most stress upon a good shape) sensible (a little learning will do), well bred (but she must have an aversion to the word *ton*), chaste and tender (I am an enthusiast in my notions of fidelity and fondness), of some good nature, a great deal of generosity (she must neither love money nor scolding, for I dislike equally a termagant and an economist). In politics, I am indifferent what side she may be of; I think I have arguments that will easily convert her to mine. As to religion, a moderate stock will satisfy me. She must believe in God and hate a saint. But as to fortune, the larger stock of that the better.

To John Laurens, Middlebrook,
New Jersey, April 1779

Foreign Influence

❦ ❧

Foreign influence is truly the GRECIAN HORSE to a republic. We cannot be too careful to exclude its entrance.

"Pacificus No. VI," Philadelphia,
July 17, 1793

The general security of nations has established it as a sacred and inviolable maxim, forming an essential bulwark of their internal

tranquility, that no agent of a foreign sovereign shall on any pretext attempt to create a schism between the citizens and the
rulers of a state, whatever be its form of government, whether
despotic or free, monarchical or republican.

"No Jacobin No. VIII," Philadelphia,
August 26, 1793

Nations are never content to confine their rivalships and enmi-
ties to themselves. It is their usual policy to disseminate them as
widely as they can regardless how far it may interfere with the
tranquility or happiness of the nations which they are able to influence.

"The Defence No. I," New York,
July 22, 1795

We are laboring hard to establish in this country principles more
and more *national* and free from all *foreign ingredients* so that we
may be neither *"Greeks nor Trojans"* but truly Americans.

To Rufus King, New York,
December 16, 1796

Foreign Intrigue

Foreign intrigues and machinations are among the most formi-
dable enemies which republics have to encounter.

"No Jacobin No. VII," Philadelphia, August 23, 1793

Foreign Investment

There may be persons disposed to look with a jealous eye on the
introduction of foreign capital as if it were an instrument to de-

prive our own citizens of the profits of our own industry. But perhaps there never could be a more unreasonable jealousy. Instead of being viewed as a rival, it ought to be considered as a most valuable auxiliary, conducing to put in motion a greater quantity of productive labor and a greater portion of useful enterprise than could exist without it.

Report on the Subject of Manufactures,
Philadelphia, December 5, 1791

Foreign Policy

❦

The neutral and the pacific policy appear to me to mark the true path to the U States.

To Edward Carrington, Philadelphia, May 26, 1792

The greater rule of our foreign politics ought to be to have as little political connections as possible with foreign nations.

Abstract of Points to Form an Address,
New York, May 16-July 5, 1796

France

❦

There is no country I have a greater curiosity to see or which I am persuaded would be so interesting to me as yours.

To Vicomte de Noailles,
April-June 1782

The conduct of France from the commencement of her successes has by gradual developments betrayed a spirit of universal domination; an opinion that she has a right to be the legislatrix of nations; that they are all bound to submit to her mandates, to take from her their moral political and religious creeds; that her plastic and regenerating hand is to mold them into whatever shape she thinks fit and that her interest is to be the sole measure of the rights of the rest of the world.

"The Warning No. I," New York, January 27, 1797

The man who . . . shall be the apologist of France and the calumniator of his own government is not an American. The choice for him lies between being deemed a fool, a madman, or a traitor.

"The Warning No. VI," New York, March 27, 1797

Like the prophet of Mecca, the tyrants of France press forward with the Koran of their faith in one hand and the sword in the other. They proselyte, subjugate, and debase. No distinction is made between republic and monarchy. All must alike yield to the aggrandizement of the "GREAT NATION."

"The Stand No. III," New York, April 7, 1798

France, swelled to a gigantic size and aping ancient Rome, except in her virtues, plainly meditates the control of mankind and is actually giving the law to nations.

"The Stand No. III," New York, April 7, 1798

Freedom

Our countrymen have all the folly of the ass and all the passiveness of the sheep in their compositions. They are determined not to be free and they can neither be frightened, discouraged, nor persuaded to change their resolution.

To John Laurens, Ramapo, New Jersey, June 30, 1780

Free Enterprise

꩜

Industry will succeed and prosper in proportion as it is left to the exertions of individual enterprise. This favorite dogma, when taken as a general rule, is true; but as an exclusive one, it is false and leads to error in the administration of public affairs.

"The Examination Number III,"
New York, March 19, 1802

Free Government

꩜

A free government [is] to be preferred to an absolute monarchy, not because of the occasional violations of *liberty* or *property*, but because of the tendency of the free government to interest the passions of the community in its favor [and thus] beget public spirit and public confidence.

Speech at Constitutional Convention,
Philadelphia, June 1-26, 1787

Free Trade

꩜

The maxims of the U States have hitherto favored a free intercourse with all the world. They have conceived that they had nothing to fear from the unrestrained competition of commercial enterprise and have only desired to be admitted to it upon equal terms.

"The Defence No. X," New York, August 26, 1795

French Army Officers

❧

Congress in the beginning went upon a very injudicious plan with respect to Frenchmen. To every adventurer that came, without even the shadow of credentials, they gave the rank of field officers.

To William Duer, Morristown, New Jersey, May 6, 1777

It is become almost proverbial in the mouths of the French officers and other foreigners that they have nothing more to do to obtain whatever they please than to assume a high tone and assert their own merit with confidence and perseverance.

To George Clinton, Valley Forge,
Pennsylvania, February 13, 1778

The French Revolution

❧

Would to heaven that we could discern in the mirror of French affairs the same humanity, the same decorum, the same gravity, the same order, the same dignity, the same solemnity which distinguished the course of the American Revolution. Clouds and darkness would not then rest upon the issue as they now do.

To —, Philadelphia,
May 18, 1793

[The French Revolution has been] one volcano succeeding another, the last still more dreadful than the former, spreading ruin and devastation far and wide, subverting the foundations of right, security, and property, of order, morality and religion; sparing neither sex nor age; confounding innocence with guilt;

involving the old and the young, the sage and the madman, the long tried friend of virtue and his country and the upstart pretender to purity and patriotism, the bold projector of the new treasons with the obscure in indiscriminate and profuse destruction.

The French Revolution,
Philadelphia, 1794

The French Revolution is a political convulsion that in a great or less degree shakes the whole civilized world, and it is of real consequence to the principles and of course to the happiness of a nation to estimate it rightly.

The French Revolution,
Philadelphia, 1794

This [new philosophy] . . . in France . . . has hurried her headlong through a rapid succession of dreadful revolutions which have laid waste property, made havoc among the arts, overthrown cities, desolated provinces, unpeopled regions, crimsoned her soil with blood, and deluged it in crime, poverty, and wretchedness; and all this as yet for no better purpose than to erect on the ruins of former things a despotism unlimited and uncontrolled; leaving to a deluded, an abused, a plundered, a scourged, and an oppressed people not even the shadow of liberty to console them for a long train of substantial misfortunes, of bitter sufferings.

Views on the French Revolution, 1794

The Future

If we look forward to a period not far distant, we shall perceive that the productions of our country will infinitely exceed the demands which Great Britain and her connections can possibly have for them; and as we shall then be greatly advanced in population, our wants will be proportionately increased.

The Farmer Refuted, New York, February 23, 1775

Gambling

Gambling, a vice destructive to the reputation of an army, and fraught with every evil not only to those who suffer themselves to engage in it, but to the army in which it is tolerated, is strictly prohibited.

General Orders, New York, January 10, 1800

Gardening

A disappointed politician you know is very apt to take refuge in a garden.

To Richard Peters, New York, December 29, 1802

Generals

Who can better judge of the bravery of a general than the soldiers under his immediate command?

To Vicomte de Noailles, November-December 1781

Government

Nothing is more common than for a free people in times of heat and violence to gratify momentary passions by letting into the government principles and precedents which afterwards prove fatal to themselves.

A Letter from Phocion, New York,
January 1-27, 1784

That honesty is still the best policy, that justice and moderation are the surest supports of every government, are maxims, which, however they may be called trite, [are] at all times true, though too seldom regarded, but rarely neglected with impunity.

A Letter from Phocion, New York,
January 1-27, 1784

It is an axiom that governments form manners as well as manners form governments.

Second Letter from Phocion, New York, April 1784

No government could give us tranquility and happiness at home which did not possess sufficient stability and strength to make us respectable abroad.

Speech at Constitutional Convention,
Philadelphia, June 29, 1787

Unless your government is respectable, foreigners will invade your rights; and to maintain tranquillity it must be respectable; even to observe neutrality, you must have a strong government.

Speech at Constitutional Convention,
Philadelphia, June 29, 1787

Why has government been instituted at all? Because the passions of men will not conform to the dictates of reason and justice without constraint.

The Federalist No. 15, New York,
December 1, 1787

Wise politicians will be cautious about fettering the government with restrictions that cannot be observed because they know that every breach of the fundamental laws, though dictated by necessity, impairs that sacred reverence which ought to be maintained in the breasts of rulers towards the constitution of a country and forms a precedent for other breaches, where the same plea of necessity does not exist at all or is less urgent and palpable.

The Federalist No. 25, New York,
December 21, 1787

Every government ought to contain in itself the means of its own preservation.

The Federalist No. 59, New York,
February 22, 1788

The true test of a good government is its aptitude and tendency to produce a good administration.

The Federalist No. 68, New York, March 12, 1788

Nothing is so dangerous to a government as to be wanting either in self confidence or self respect.

Opinion on the Brigantine *Little Sarah*,
Philadelphia, July 8, 1793

Government is frequently and aptly classed under two descriptions, a government of FORCE and a government of LAWS; the first is the definition of despotism, the last of liberty.

"Tully No. III," Philadelphia, August 28, 1794

Government being administered by men is naturally like individuals, subject to particular impulses, passions, prejudices, vices; of course, to inconstancy of views and mutability of conduct.

Report on Public Credit, Philadelphia, January 16, 1795

A weak and embarrassed government never fails to be unpopular.

The Defence of the Funding System,
New York, July 1795

Cherish the actual government. It is the government of our own choice, free in its [principles], the guardian of our common rights, the patron of our common interests, and containing within itself a provision for its own amendment.

Abstract of Points to Form an Address,
New York, May 16-July 5, 1796

No plan of governing is well founded which does not regard man as a compound of selfish and virtuous passions.

Draft of George Washington's Eighth Annual Address
To Congress, New York, November 10, 1796

Whenever the government appears in arms, it ought to appear like a *Hercules* and inspire respect by the display of strength.

To James McHenry, New York, March 18, 1799

Every species of government has its specific principles. Ours perhaps are more peculiar than those of any other in the universe. *It is a composition of the freest principles of the English Constitution*, with others, derived from natural right and reason. To these nothing can be more opposed than the maxims of absolute monarchies.

"The Examination Number VII,"
New York, January 7, 1802

Government Action

❧ ❧

The government must take care not to appear pusillanimous.

To Oliver Wolcott, Jr., New York, April 20, 1796

In an emergency like the present, energy is wisdom.

To Charles Cotesworth Pinckney,
New York, December 29, 1802

Government Influence

❧ ❧

The government of a country cannot altogether change either the taste or the disposition of a people, but its influence may check or cherish it.

Conversation with George Beckwith,
New York, October 1789

Government Obligations

❧ ❧

An individual may plead duress and compulsion as an objection to the performance of his engagements, but this is impossible to a government.

The Defence of the Funding System,
New York, July 1795

Government Salaries

※ ※

If then it be essential to the prosperous course of every government that it shall be able to command the services of its most able and most virtuous citizens of every class, it follows that the compensations which our government allows ought to be revised and materially increased. The character and success of republican government appear absolutely to depend on this policy.

Draft of George Washington's Eighth Annual
Address to Congress, New York,
November 10, 1796

Great Britain

※ ※

She is an obstinate old dame and seems determined to ruin her whole family rather than to let Miss America go on flirting with her new lovers, with whom, as giddy young girls often do, she eloped in contempt of her mother's authority.

To Elizabeth Schuyler, Teaneck,
New Jersey, August 1780

I believe the British government forms the best model the world ever produced. . . . This government has for its object *public strength* and *individual security*.

Speech at Constitutional Convention,
Philadelphia, June 18, 1787

I think the British government is the only proper one for such an extensive Country [as ours]. This government unites the highest public strength with the most perfect individual security.

> Speech at Constitutional Convention,
> Philadelphia, June 18, 1787

I have always preferred a connection with [Great Britain] to that of any other country. We think in English and have a similarity of prejudices and of predilections.

> Conversation with George Beckwith,
> New York, October 1789

A proper estimate of the operation of the human passions must satisfy us that she [Great Britain] would be less disposed to receive the law from us than from any other nation, a people recently become a nation, not long since one of her dependencies, and as yet, if a Hercules, a Hercules in the cradle.

> To George Washington, Philadelphia, April 14, 1794

Guerrilla Warfare

The circumstances of our country put it in our power to evade a pitched battle. It will be better policy to harass and exhaust the soldiery [of Great Britain] by frequent skirmishes and incursions than to take the open field with them, by which means they would have the full benefit of their superior regularity and skill.

> *The Farmer Refuted*, New York, February 23, 1775

PLUNDER and devastations ever march in the train of irregulars.

> *The Federalist No. 8*, New York, November 20, 1787

Elizabeth Schuyler Hamilton

✺

She is most unmercifully handsome and so perverse that she has none of those pretty affectations which are the prerogatives of beauty. Her good sense is destitute of that happy mixture of vanity and ostentation which would make it conspicuous to the whole tribe of fools and foplings as well as to men of understanding. . . . In short she is so strange a creature that she possesses all the beauties, virtues, and graces of her sex without any of those amiable defects which from their general prevalence are esteemed by connoisseurs necessary shades in the character of a fine woman.

To Margarita Schuyler, Morristown,
New Jersey, February 1780

Next fall completes my doom. I give up my liberty to Miss Schuyler. She is a good hearted girl who I am sure will never play the termagant; though not a genius she has fine black eyes; is rather handsome and has every other requisite of the exterior to make a lover happy. And believe me, I am lover in earnest, though I do not speak of the perfections of my Mistress in the enthusiasm of chivalry.

To John Laurens, Ramapo,
New Jersey, June 30, 1780

I love you more and more every hour. The sweet softness and delicacy of your mind and manners, the elevation of your sentiments, the real goodness of your heart, its tenderness to me, the beauties of your face and person, your unpretending good sense, and that innocent simplicity and frankness which pervade your actions—all these appear to me with increasing amiableness and place you in my estimation above all the rest of your sex.

To Elizabeth Schuyler, Preakness,
New Jersey, July 2-4, 1780

You are certainly a little sorceress and have bewitched me, for you have made me disrelish everything that used to please me, and have rendered me as restless and unsatisfied with all about me as if I was the inhabitant of another world and had nothing in common with this [one].

To Elizabeth Schuyler,
Dobbs Ferry, New York,
August 8, 1780

My heart looks forward with delicious anticipation to the period of our reunion.

To Elizabeth Hamilton,
Albany, New York,
February 10, 1800

Happiness

Every nation has a right to carve out its own happiness in its own way, and it is the height of presumption in another, to attempt to fashion its political creed.

To George Washington,
Philadelphia, May 2, 1793

Experience more and more convinces me that true happiness is only to be found in the bosom of one's own family.

To Elizabeth Hamilton,
Albany, New York,
October 25, 1801

Harsh Words

Hard words are very rarely useful in public proceedings.

To Oliver Wolcott, Jr., New York, June 6, 1797

Honesty

One great error is that we suppose mankind more honest than they are.

Speech at Constitutional Convention,
Philadelphia, June 22, 1787

Honor

True honor is a rational thing. It is as distinguishable from Quixotism as true courage from the spirit of a bravo.

"The Defence No. V," New York,
August 5, 1795

The honor of a nation is its life. Deliberately to abandon it is to commit an act of political suicide.

"The Warning No. III," New York,
February 21, 1797

Human Affairs

❧ ❧

There must be a portion of nonsense in human affairs.

> To Jeremiah Wadsworth, Philadelphia,
> April 12, 1791

Human Nature

❧ ❧

The safest reliance of every government is on men's interests. This is a principle of human nature on which all political speculation, to be just, must be founded.

> *A Letter from Phocion*, New York,
> January 1-27, 1784

The supposition of universal venality in human nature is little less an error in political reasoning than the supposition of universal rectitude.

> *The Federalist No. 76*, New York,
> April 1, 1788

It may seem strange to some that a man who had behaved well in one situation should be so entirely defective or faulty in another. But when acquainted with human nature and its history on a large scale, [anyone] will be sensible that there is nothing extraordinary in the thing. Many of those who have proved the worst scourges of society have, in the commencement of their career, been its brightest ornaments. These fair beginnings are sometimes the effect of premeditation to pave the way to future mischief; at other times, they are the natural result of a mixed character placed in favorable circumstances.

> "H. G. Letter IV," New York,
> February 24, 1789

'Tis the lot of every thing human to mingle a portion of ill with the good.

To Rufus King, Philadelphia,
July 8, 1791

Experience teaches that men are often so much governed by what they are accustomed to see and practice that the simplest and most obvious improvements in the [most] ordinary occupations are adopted with hesitation, reluctance, and by slow gradations.

Report on the Subject of Manufactures,
Philadelphia, December 5, 1791

Men are rather reasoning rather tha[n] reasonable animals, for the most part governed by the impulse of passion.

To James A. Bayard, New York,
April 16-21, 1802

Hurricane

It seemed as if a total dissolution of nature was taking place. The roaring of the sea and wind, fiery meteors flying about it in the air, the prodigious glare of almost perpetual lightening, the crash of the falling houses, and the ear-piercing shrieks of the distressed, were sufficient to strike astonishment into Angels.

To Royal Danish American Gazette,
St. Croix, September 6, 1772

Death comes rushing on in triumph veiled in a mantle of tenfold darkness. His unrelenting scythe, pointed and ready for the stroke. On his right hand sits destruction, hurling the winds and belching forth flames. Calamity on his left, threatening famine, disease, and distress of all kinds.

To *Royal Danish American Gazette*,
St. Croix, September 6, 1772

Immigration

❧ ⚘

To find pleasure in the calamities of other nations would be criminal; but to benefit ourselves by opening an asylum to those who suffer in consequence of them is as justifiable as it is pol[itic].

Report on the Subject of Manufactures,
Philadelphia, December 5, 1791

The United States have already felt the evils of incorporating a large number of foreigners into their national mass; it has served very much to divide the community and to distract our councils by promoting in different classes different predilections in favor of particular foreign nations and antipathies against others.

"The Examination Number VIII,"
New York, January 12, 1802

Impeachment

❧ ⚘

A well constituted court for the trial of impeachments is an object not more to be desired than difficult to be obtained in a government wholly elective. The subjects of its jurisdiction are those offenses which proceed from the misconduct of public men, or, in other words, from the abuse or violation of some public trust. They are of a nature which may with peculiar propriety be denominated POLITICAL, as they relate chiefly to injuries done immediately to the society itself. The prosecution of them, for this reason, will seldom fail to agitate the passions of the whole community, and to divide it into parties, more or less friendly or inimical to the accused. In many cases, it will connect itself with the pre-existing factions and will enlist all their animosities, partialities, influence, and interest on one side or on the other; and in such cases there will always be the greatest danger that the decision will be regulated more by the comparative strength of parties than by the real demonstrations of innocence or guilt.

The Federalist No. 65, New York, March 7, 1788

Implied Powers

❧ ☙

Every power vested in a government is in its nature *sovereign* and includes by *force* of the *term* a right to employ all the *means* requisite and fairly *applicable* to the attainment of the ends of such power; and which are not precluded by restrictions and exceptions specified in the Constitution; or not immoral or not contrary to the essential ends of political society.

Opinion on Constitutionality of an
Act to Establish a National Bank,
Philadelphia, February 23, 1791

It is not denied that there are *implied* as well as *express* powers and that the former are as effectually delegated as the latter.

Opinion on Constitutionality of an
Act to Establish a National Bank,
Philadelphia, February 23, 1791

Wherever an *end* is granted, the *usual* and *proper means* of enjoying it are implied in the grant.

"The Defence No. XI," New York, August 28, 1795

Independence

❧

Peace made, my dear friend, a new scene opens. The object then will be to make our independence a blessing. To do this we must secure our *union* on solid foundations; an herculean task and to effect which mountains of prejudice must be leveled!

To John Laurens, Albany, New York, August 15, 1782

Industry and Frugality

❧

Cultivate also industry and frugality. They are auxiliaries of good morals and great sources of private and national prosperity.

Draft of George Washington's Farewell Address, New York, July 30, 1796

Inheritance

❧

The present law of inheritance, making an equal division among the children of the parent's property, will soon melt down those great estates, which if they continued might favor the power of the *few*.

Second Letter from Phocion, New York, April 1784

Institutions

It is the lot of all human institutions, even those of the most perfect kind, to have defects as well as excellencies, ill as well as good propensities. This results from the imperfection of the institutor, Man.

"The Defence No. I," New York, July 22, 1795

The utility of every institution depends on the competency of the agents who are to execute it.

Report on Revenue, Philadelphia, January 31, 1795

Integrity

I trust that I shall always be able to bear, as I ought, imputations of error of judgment; but I acknowledge that I cannot be entirely patient under charges which impeach the integrity of my public motives or conduct.

To George Washington, Philadelphia, August 18, 1792

Interest Rates

The natural effect of low interest is to increase trade and industry because undertakings of every kind can be prosecuted with greater advantage. . . . Everything, therefore, which tends to lower the rate of interest is peculiarly worthy of the cares of legislators.

Report on a National Bank, Philadelphia, December 14, 1790

International Blame

❧

Nothing is more common in disputes between nations than [for] each side to charge the other with being the aggressor or delinquent.

"The Defence No. III," New York, July 29, 1795

International Compromise

❧

Reject the principle of compromise and the feuds of nations must become much more deadly than they have heretofore been. There would scarcely ever be room for the adjustment of differences without an appeal to the sword; and when drawn, it would seldom be sheathed but with the destruction of one or the other party. The earth, now too often stained, would then continually stream with human gore.

"The Defence No. III," New York, July 29, 1795

International Law

❧

'Tis clear that no foreign nation can without the consent of our government *organize* within our territory and jurisdiction the means of military expeditions by land or sea. To do it is an offense against the law of nations; the law of nations is a part of the law of the land.

To Richard Harison, Philadelphia, June 13-15, 1793

Intolerance

❧ ❧

There is bigotry in politics, as well as in religions, equally pernicious in both. The zealots of either description are ignorant of the advantage of a spirit of toleration.

Second Letter from Phocion, New York, April 1784

Jealousy

❧ ❧

Jealousy is a predominant passion of human nature and is a source of the greatest evils. Whenever it takes place between rulers and their subjects, it proves the bane of civil society.

The Farmer Refuted, New York,
February 23, 1775

Thomas Jefferson

❧ ❧

In France . . . he drank deeply of the French philosophy in religion, in science, in politics.

To Edward Carrington, Philadelphia,
May 26, 1792

He came electrified *plus* with attachment to France and with the project of knitting together the two countries in the closest political bands.

To Edward Carrington, Philadelphia, May 26, 1792

Mr. Jefferson is emulous of being the head of a party whose politics have constantly aimed at elevating state power upon the ruins of national authority.

"An American No. I," Philadelphia, August 4, 1792

Mr. Jefferson's politics, whatever may be the motives of them, *tend* to national disunion, insignificance, disorder, and discredit.

"Catullus No. III," Philadelphia,
September 29, 1792

Mr. Jefferson has hitherto been distinguished as the quiet, modest, retiring philosopher, as the plain, simple, unambitious republican. He shall not now for the first time be regarded as the intriguing incendiary, the aspiring turbulent competitor.

"Catullus No. III," Philadelphia,
September 29, 1792

There is always "a *first time*" when characters studious of artful disguises are unveiled; when the vizor of stoicism is plucked from the brow of the epicurean; when the plain garb of Quaker simplicity is stripped from the concealed voluptuary; when Caesar *coyly refusing* the proffered diadem is seen to be Caesar *rejecting* the trappings but tenaciously grasping the substance of imperial domination.

"Catullus No. III," Philadelphia,
September 29, 1792

I admit that his politics are tinctured with fanaticism, that he is too much in earnest in his democracy, that he has been a mischievous enemy to the principle measures of our past administration, that he is crafty and persevering in his objects, that he is not scrupulous about the means of success, nor very mindful of truth, and that he is a contemptible hypocrite.

To James A. Bayard, New York, January 16, 1801

He is as likely as any man I know to temporize—to calculate what will be likely to promote his own reputation and advantage.

To James A. Bayard, New York, January 16, 1801

Jefferson and Aaron Burr

❧ ☙

Jefferson or *Burr?*—the former without all doubt. The latter in my judgment has no principle public or private, could be bound by no agreement, will listen to no monitor but his ambition; and for this purpose will use the *worst* part of the community as a ladder to climb to perman[en]t power and an instrument to crush the better part.

To Gouverneur Morris, New York,
December 24, 1800

Jefferson and James Madison

❧ ☙

Mr. Madison cooperating with Mr. Jefferson is at the head of a faction decidedly hostile to me and my administration and actuated by views in my judgment subversive of the principles of good government and dangerous to the union, peace, and happiness of the Country.

To Edward Carrington, Philadelphia,
May 26, 1792

They have a womanish attachment to France and a womanish resentment against Great Britain.

To Edward Carrington, Philadelphia, May 26, 1792

They forget an old but a very just though a coarse saying, that it is much easier to raise the Devil than to lay him.

To Edward Carrington, Philadelphia,
May 26, 1792

Jeffersonian Republicans

❧

Such a collection of blotched reputations need but be exposed to excite horror. If the tree known by its fruit, why not the fruit by the tree? If the fountain [is] corrupt, how can pure waters be expected to flow from it? Has rottenness entered into the heart, how can the blood remain untainted?

"Hambden," Kingston, New York,
August 30, 1800

Jefferson's Presidency

❧

The prospects of our country are not brilliant. The mass is far from sound. At headquarters a most visionary theory presides. Depend upon it, this is the fact to a great extreme. No army, no navy, no *active* commerce; national defence not by arms but by embargoes; prohibition of trade, etc.; as little government as possible within—these are the pernicious dreams which as far and as fast as possible will be attempted to be realized.

To Rufus King, New York,
June 3, 1802

Jews

❧ ❧

[The] progress of the Jews . . . from their earliest history to the present time has been and is entirely out of the *ordinary course* of human affairs. Is it not then a fair conclusion that the *cause* also is an *extraordinary one*—in other words, that it is the effect of some great providential plan? The man who will draw this conclusion will look for the solution in the Bible. He who will not draw it ought to give us another fair solution.

Comments on Jews, n.p., n.d.

Judges

❧ ❧

It cannot be denied that every permanent body of men is, more or less, liable to be influenced by the spirit of the existing administration, that such a body may be liable to corruption, and that they may be inclined to lean over towards party modes.

Speech in People v. Croswell, Albany, New York,
February 14-15, 1804

Judicial Review

❧ ❧

Laws are a dead letter without courts to expound and define their true meaning and operation.

The Federalist No. 22, New York,
December 14, 1787

The interpretation of the laws is the proper and peculiar province of the courts. A constitution is in fact and must be regarded by the judges as a fundamental law. It therefore belongs to them to ascertain its meaning as well as the meaning of any particular act proceeding from the legislative body.

The Federalist No. 78, New York,
May 28, 1788

Judicial Tyranny

❧ ☙

Never can tyranny be introduced into this country by arms; these can never get rid of a popular spirit of enquiry; the only way to crush it down is by a servile tribunal. It is only by the abuse of the forms of justice that we can be enslaved.

Speech in *People v. Croswell*,
Albany, New York,
February 14-15, 1804

Labor

❧ ☙

We labor less now than any civilized nation of Europe, and a habit of labor in the people is as essential to the health and vigor of their minds and bodies as it is conducive to the welfare of the state.

To Robert Morris, De Peyster's Point,
New York, April 30, 1781

The Law

❧ ❧

The most obvious or popular sense of the words of a law are always of great force in their construction.

Circular to the Collectors of the Customs,
Philadelphia, November 30, 1789

The idea of pursuing *legal* measures to *obstruct* the *operation* of a *law* needs little comment. Legal measures may be pursued to procure the repeal of a law, but to *obstruct its operation* presents a contradiction in terms. The *operation*, or what is the same thing, the *execution* of a *law* cannot be *obstructed* after it has been constitutionally enacted without illegality and crime.

To George Washington, Philadelphia,
August 5, 1794

Resistance [to the law] is treason against society, against liberty, against everything that ought to be dear to a free, enlightened, and prudent people. To tolerate [it is] to abandon your most precious interests. Not to subdue it [is] to tolerate it.

"Tully No. III," Philadelphia,
August 28, 1794

It is a very precious and important idea that those who are called out in support and defense of the laws should not give occasion or even pretext to impute to them infractions of the laws.

To Thomas Mifflin, Pennsylvania,
October 19, 1794

There is no alternative: we must be ruled by municipal law or by a military force.

Speech on Repeal of the Judiciary Act,
New York, February 11, 1802

Leadership

❧ ❧

I shall proceed under an impression that my constituents expect from me the free exercise of my judgment and the free declaration of my sentiments.

Speech in New York Assembly, New York, January 19, 1787

Leniency

❧ ❧

Though severity towards offenders is to be avoided as much as can consist with the safety of society; yet impunity in such cases is apt to produce too much promptitude in setting the laws at defiance.

To Thomas Sim Lee, Philadelphia, September 24, 1794

Liberty

❧ ❧

No person that has enjoyed the sweets of liberty can be insensible of its infinite value or can reflect on its reverse without horror and detestation.

A Full Vindication of the Measures of Congress,
New York, December 15, 1774

Remember civil and religious liberty always go together; if the foundation of the one be sapped, the other will fall.

A Full Vindication of the Measures of Congress,
New York, December 15, 1774

There is a certain enthusiasm in liberty that makes human nature rise above itself in acts of bravery and heroism.

The Farmer Refuted, New York,
February 23, 1775

I consider civil liberty in a genuine unadulterated sense as the greatest of terrestrial blessings. I am convinced that the whole human race is entitled to it; and that it can be wrested from no part of them without the blackest and most aggravated guilt.

The Farmer Refuted, New York,
February 23, 1775

The liberties of America are an infinite stake. We should not play a desperate game for it or put it upon the issue of a single cast of the die.

To Robert R. Livingston, New Jersey, June 28, 1777

The security therefore of the public liberty must consist in such a distribution of the sovereign power as will make it morally impossible for one part to gain an ascendency over the others or for the whole to unite in a scheme of usurpation.

"The Continentalist No. II," Fishkill,
New York, July 19, 1781

The meaning of the word *liberty* has been contested. Its true sense must be the enjoyment of the common privileges of subjects under the same government.

A Letter from Phocion, New York, January 1-27, 1784

The world has its eye upon America. The noble struggle we have made in the cause of liberty has occasioned a kind of revolution in human sentiment. The influence of our example has penetrated the gloomy regions of despotism and has pointed the way to inquiries which may shake it to its deepest foundations.

Second Letter from Phocion, New York, April 1784

In all struggles for liberty, the leaders of the people have fallen under two principal discriminations: those who, to a conviction of the real usefulness of civil liberty, join a sincere attachment to the public good; and those who are of restless and turbulent spirits, impatient of constraint, averse to all power or superiority which they do not themselves enjoy. With men of the latter description, the transition from demagogues to despots is neither difficult nor uncommon.

"H. G. Letter IV," New York,
February 24, 1789

A struggle for liberty is in itself respectable and glorious. When conducted with magnanimity, justice, and humanity, it ought to command the admiration of every friend to human nature. But if sullied by crimes and extravagancies, it loses its respectability. Though success may rescue it from infamy, it cannot in the opinion of the sober part of Mankind attach to it much positive merit or praise. But in the event of a want of success, a general execration must attend it.

To George Washington, Philadelphia, May 2, 1793

I trust there is enough of virtue and good sense in the people of America to baffle every attempt against their prosperity—though masked under the specious garb of an extraordinary zeal for liberty. They practically, I doubt not, adopt this sacred maxim, that without government there is no true liberty.

To —, Philadelphia, May 18, 1793

To subvert by force republican liberty in this Country, nothing short of entire conquest would suffice.

"Americanus No. II," Philadelphia,
February 7, 1794

The love of Liberty is here the ruling passion *of the Citizens of the Ustates*, pervading every class animating every bosom.

The French Revolution, Philadelphia, 1794

True liberty, by protecting the exertions of talents and industry and securing to them their justly acquired fruits, tends more powerfully than any other cause to augment the mass of national wealth and to produce the mischiefs of opulence.

The Defence of the Funding System,
New York, July 1795

Local Interests

❧ ☙

I hold it that different societies have all different views and interests to pursue and always prefer local to general concerns.

Speech at Constitutional Convention,
Philadelphia, June 18, 1787

Loss of a Child

❧ ☙

[It was] beyond comparison the most afflicting of my life. . . . The highest as well as the eldest hope of my family has been taken from me.

To Benjamin Rush, New York,
March 29, 1802

Louisiana Purchase

❧ ☙

Sound policy unquestionably demanded of us to begin with a prompt, bold, and vigorous resistance against the injustice; to seize the object at once; and having this *vantage ground*, should we have thought it advisable to terminate hostilities by a purchase, we might then have done it on almost our own terms.

"Purchase of Louisiana," New York,
July 5, 1803

On the whole, we think it may with candor be said that whether the possession at this time of any territory west of the river Mississippi will be advantageous is at best extremely problematical. For ourselves, we are very much inclined to the opinion that, after all, it is the island of N. Orleans, by which the command of a free navigation of the Mississippi is secured, that gives to this interesting cession its greatest value and will render it in every view of immense benefit to our country.

"Purchase of Louisiana," New York,
July 5, 1803

Love

❧ ☙

ALL FOR LOVE is my motto.

To Catherine Livingston, Morristown,
New Jersey, May 1777

Love is a sort of insanity, and everything I write savors strongly of it.

To Elizabeth Schuyler, Preakness,
New Jersey, October 13, 1780

While all other passions decline in me, those of love and friendship gain new strength.

To Elizabeth Hamilton, Albany,
New York, January 26, 1800

Love Letter

✣

I cannot tell you what ecstasy I felt in casting my eye over the sweet effusions of tenderness it contains. My Betsey's soul speaks in every line and bids me be the happiest of mortals. I am so and will be so.

To Elizabeth Schuyler, Amboy,
New Jersey, March 17, 1780

Loyalty

✣

It is a known fact in human nature that its affections are commonly weak in proportion to the distance or diffusiveness of the object. Upon the same principle that a man is more attached to his family than to his neighborhood, to his neighborhood than to the community at large, the people of each state would be apt to feel a stronger bias towards their local governments than towards the government of the Union; unless the force of that principle should be destroyed by a much better administration of the latter.

The Federalist No. 17, New York,
December 5, 1787

Luxury

✣

Luxury has arrived to a great pitch; and it is a universal maxim that luxury indicates the declension of a state.

A Full Vindication of the Measures of Congress,
New York, December 15, 1774

Mankind

❧ ❧

Mankind are forever destined to be the dupes of bold and cunning imposture.

> To Charles Cotesworth Pinckney,
> The Grange, New York,
> December 29, 1802

Manufactures

❧ ❧

The establishment of manufactures in the United States, when maturely considered, will be fo[und] to be of the highest importance to their prosperity. It [is] an almost self evident proposition that that com[muni]ty which can most completely supply its own w[ants] is in a state of the highest political perfection. [And] both theory and experience conspire to prove that a nation (unless from a very peculiar coincidence of circumstances) cannot possess much *active* wealth but as the result of extensive manufactures.

> Prospectus of Society for Establishing
> Useful Manufactures, Philadelphia,
> August, 1791

Manufactures open a wider field to exertions of ingenuity than agriculture; it would not be a strained conjecture that the labor employed in the former, being at once more constant, more uniform, and more ingenious than that which is employed in the latter, will be found at the same time more productive.

> *Report on the Subject of Manufactures*,
> Philadelphia, December 5, 1791

Not only the wealth, but the independence and security, of a country appear to be materially connected with the prosperity of manufactures.

Report on the Subject of Manufactures,
Philadelphia, December 5, 1791

It may hereafter deserve legislative consideration whether manufactories of all the necessary weapons of war ought not to be established on account of the government itself. . . . As a general rule, manufactories on the immediate account of government are to be avoided; but this seems to be one of the few exceptions which that rule admits, depending on very special reasons.

Report on the Subject of Manufactures,
Philadelphia, December 5, 1791

When a manufacture is in its infancy, it is impolitic to tax it because the tax would be both unproductive and would add to the difficulties which naturally impede the first attempts to establish a new manufacture so as to endanger its success. But when a manufacture (as in the case of distilled spirits in the United States) is arrived at maturity, it is as fit an article of taxation as any other.

Report on Distilled Spirits, Philadelphia,
March 5, 1792

As a general rule manufactories carried on upon public account are to be avoided. But every general rule may admit of exceptions.

Draft of George Washington's Eighth
Annual Address to Congress,
New York, November 10, 1796

Marriage

'Tis a very good thing when their stars unite two people who are fit for each other, who have souls capable of relishing the sweets of friendship and sensibilities.

To Margarita Schuyler, New Windsor,
New York, January 21, 1781

Merchants

The good will of the merchants is very important in many senses, and if it can be secured [by government officials] without any improper sacrifice or introducing a looseness of practice, it is desirable to do it.

To Jeremiah Olney, Philadelphia,
April 2, 1793

I regret much every embarrassment which is experienced by the mercantile body—whether arising from the public operations, from accidental and unavoidable causes, or from a spirit of enterprise beyond the capital which is to support it. That valuable class of citizens forms too important an organ of the general weal not to claim every practicable and reasonable exemption and indulgence.

To John Brown, Philadelphia,
April 5, 1793

Every merchant is a *speculator* by the nature of his calling.

To the Citizens of New York, New York,
December 12, 1796

Merit

One of the best and most useful feelings of the human heart [is] a reverence for merit.

> Defense of the President's Neutrality Proclamation,
> Philadelphia, May 1793

Military Academy

A Military Academy instituted on proper principles would serve to secure to our country, though within a narrow sp[h]ere, a solid fund of military information which would always be ready for national emergencies and would facilitate the diffusion of military knowledge as those emergenc[i]es might require.

> Draft of George Washington's Eighth Annual
> Address to Congress, New York,
> November 10, 1796

Military Discipline

A military institution must be worse than useless—it must be pernicious—if a just severity does not uphold and enforce discipline.

> To James McHenry, New York,
> May 27, 1799

Military Establishment

❧ ❧

That in proportion as the circumstan[ces] and policy of a country forbid a large military establishment, it is important that as much perfection as possible should be given to that which may at any time exist.

> To James McHenry, New York,
> November 23, 1799

Military Organization

❧ ❧

The orderly and prosperous course of the service can only be the result of a good organization.

> To James McHenry, New York,
> May 7, 1799

Military Pride

❧ ❧

Military pride is to be excited and kept up by military parade. No time ought to be lost in teaching the recruits the use of arms.

> To James McHenry, New York,
> May 18, 1799

Military Science

❧ ❧

No sound mind can doubt the essentiality of Military Science in time of war any more than the moral certainty that the most pacific policy on the part of a government will not preserve it from being engaged in war, more or less frequently.

To James McHenry, New York,
November 23, 1799

Military Strategy

It is also a common and well grounded rule in war to strike first and principally at the capital towns and cities in order to [effect] the conquest of a country.

To the New York Committee of Correspondence,
Morristown, New Jersey, April 5, 1777

Military System

A steady system constituted by fixed rules is the essential basis of a good and prosperous military establishment.

To James McHenry, New York,
September 27, 1799

Military Tradition

Military prejudices are not only inseparable from, but they are essential to the military profession. The government which desires to have a satisfied and useful army must consult them. They cannot be molded at its pleasure. It is vain to aim at it.

To James McHenry, New York,
September 19, 1799

Military Uniforms

Nothing is more necessary than to stimulate the vanity of soldiers. To this end a smart dress is essential.

To James McHenry, New York,
May 18, 1799

Militia

The militia, an excellent auxiliary for internal defence, could not be advantageously employed in distant expeditions requiring time and perseverance. For these, men regularly engaged for a competent period are indispensable.

"Americanus No. I," Philadelphia,
January 31, 1794

Mischief

There never was any mischief but had a *priest* or a woman at the bottom.

To John Laurens, West Point,
New York, September 11, 1779

Men bent upon mischief are more active in the pursuit of their object than those who aim at doing good.

A Letter from Phocion, New York,
January 1-27, 1784

Misfortune

❧ ❧

Should you ever be shut up in the seven towers or get the plague, if you are a true philosopher, you will consider this only as laughing matter.

To William Loughton Smith, New York, March 11, 1800

The Mississippi River

❧ ❧

The navigation of the Mississippi is to us an object of immense consequence. Besides other considerations connected with it, if the government of the UStates can procure and secure the enjoyment of it to our Western Country, it will be an infinitely strong link of Union between that country and the Atlantic States. As its preservation will depend on the naval resources of the Atlantic States, the Western country cannot but feel that this essential interest depends on its remaining firmly united with them.

To John Jay, Philadelphia, May 6, 1794

Mistakes

❧ ❧

In common life to retract an error, even in the beginning, is no easy task. Perseverance confirms us in it and rivets the difficulty; but in a public station, to have been in an error and to have persisted in it when it is detected, ruins both reputation and fortune. To this we may add that disappointment and opposition inflame the minds of men and attach them still more to their mistakes.

A Full Vindication of the Measures of Congress,
New York, December 15, 1774

Mobs

❧ ☙

There is no doubt that justice to the parties concerned, the maintenance of the laws, and the discouragement of a practice which attempts an usurpation of the functions of government and goes in subversion of all order requires that steps should be seriously taken to bring the offenders to justice.

To George Washington, Philadelphia, May 9, 1794

Moderation

❧ ☙

In times of such commotion as the present, while the passions of men are worked up to an uncommon pitch, there is great danger of fatal extremes. The same state of the passions which fits the multitude, who have not a sufficient stock of reason and knowledge to guide them for opposition to tyranny and oppression, very naturally leads them to a contempt and disregard of all authority. The due medium is hardly to be found among the more intelligent; it is almost impossible among the unthinking populace.

To John Jay, New York,
November 26, 1775

One may as well preach moderation to the winds as to our zealots.

To Henry Lee, Philadelphia,
June 22, 1793

Moderation in every nation is a virtue.

"The Warning No. III," New York,
February 21, 1797

Monarchy

The advantage of a monarch is this: He is above corruption; he must always intend in respect to foreign nations the true interest and glory of the people.

Speech at Constitutional Convention,
Philadelphia, June 18, 1787

Money

❧ ☙

I hate money making men.

To John Laurens, Middlebrook,
New Jersey, May 22, 1779

There is nothing men differ so readily about as the payment of money.

The Federalist No. 7, New York,
November 17, 1787

Money is with propriety considered as the vital principle of the body politic, as that which sustains its life and motion and enables it to perform its most essential functions.

The Federalist No. 30, New York,
December 28, 1787

The effects of imagination and prejudice cannot safely be disregarded in anything that relates to money.

Report on the Establishment of a Mint,
Philadelphia, January 28, 1791

Contempt and neglect must attend those who manifest that they have no principle but to get money.

To Philip Livingston, Philadelphia, April 2, 1792

Moral Decay

Opinions for a long time have been gradually gaining ground which threaten the foundations of religion, morality and society.

Views on the French Revolution, 1794

Motives

As to the motives by which I have been influenced, I leave my general conduct in private and public life to speak for them.

To George Washington, Philadelphia, August 18, 1792

The people commonly act more from their feelings than from their understandings.

To Marquis de Barbe-Marbois, New Bridge, New Jersey, September 13, 1780

National Character

Whatever refined politicians may think, it is of great consequence to preserve a national character; and if it should once seem to be a system in any state to violate its faith whenever it is the least inconvenient to keep it, it will unquestionably have an ill effect upon foreign negotiations and tend to bring government at home into contempt.

To George Clinton, Valley Forge,
Pennsylvania, March 12, 1778

It is too much characteristic of our national temper to be ingenious in finding out and magnifying the minutest disadvantages, and to reject measures of evident utility, even of necessity, to avoid trivial and sometimes imaginary evils.

"The Continentalist No. V," Fishkill,
New York, April 18, 1782

Mental debasement is the greatest misfortune that can befall a people. The most pernicious of conquests which a state can experience is a conquest over that elevated sense of its own rights, which inspires a due sensibility to insult and injury, over that virtuous pride of character which prefers any peril or sacrifice to a final submission to oppression, and which regards national ignominy as the greatest of national calamities.

"The Warning No. III," New York,
February 21, 1797

National Credit

❧ ☙

The opinion which some entertain is altogether a false one that it is more important to maintain our credit abroad than at home. The latter is far the most important nursery of resources and consequently far the most important to be inviolably maintained.

To Oliver Wolcott, Jr., Albany,
New York, April 10, 1795

National Debt

❧ ⚘

A national debt, if it is not excessive will be to us a national blessing; it will be powerful cement of our union.

> To Robert Morris, De Peyster's Point,
> New York, April 30, 1781

It is a well known fact that in countries in which the national debt is properly funded and an object of established confidence, it answers most of the purposes of money.

> *Report on Public Credit*, New York,
> January 9, 1790

Nothing can more interest the national credit and prosperity than a constant and systematic attention to husband all the means previously possessed for extinguishing the present debt and to avoid, as much as possible, the incurring of any new debt.

> Report on Additional Supplies,
> Philadelphia, March 16, 1792

[We must] prevent *that progressive accumulation of debt which must ultimately endanger* all government.

> *Report on Public Credit*, Philadelphia, January 16, 1795

To extinguish a debt which exists and to avoid contracting more are ideas almost always favored by public feeling and opinion; but to pay taxes for the one or the other purpose, which are the only means of avoiding the evil, is always more or less unpopular.

> *Report on Public Credit*, Philadelphia,
> January 16, 1795

There is a general propensity in those who administer the affairs of a government, founded in the constitution of man, to shift off the burden from the present to a future day; a propensity which may be expected to be strong in proportion as the form of the state is popular.

Report on Public Credit, Philadelphia, January 16, 1795

The creation of debt should always be accompanied with the means of extinguishment.

Report on Public Credit, Philadelphia, January 16, 1795

The true definition of public debt is *a property subsisting in the faith of the Government*. Its essence is promise. Its definite value depends upon the reliance that the promise will be definitely fulfilled.

Report on Public Credit, Philadelphia, January 16, 1795

National Disgrace

❧ ☙

It is a *sound maxim* that a state had better hazard any calamities than submit tamely to absolute disgrace.

To George Washington, New York, September 15, 1790

The nation which can prefer disgrace to danger is prepared for a master and deserves one.

"The Warning No. III," New York, February 21, 1797

It is difficult to fix the precise point at which indignity or affront from one state to another ceases to be negotiable without absolute humiliation and disgrace. It is for the most part a relative question—relative to the comparative strength of the parties, the motives for peace or war, the antecedent relations, [and] the circumstances of the moment.

To James McHenry, Albany, New York, April 29, 1798

National Gratitude

It is necessary then to reflect, however painful the reflection, that gratitude is a duty or sentiment which between nations can rarely have any solid foundation.

To George Washington, New York,
September 15, 1790

Between individuals, occasion is not unfrequently given to the exercise of gratitude. . . . But among nations they perhaps never occur. It may be affirmed as a general principle that the predominant motive of go[od] offices from one nation to another is the interest or advantage of the nations which perform them.

"Pacificus No. IV," Philadelphia,
July 10, 1793

National Interest

The primary motives of France for the assistance which she gave us [during the American Revolution] was obviously to enfeeble a hated and powerful rival by breaking in pieces the British Empire. A secondary motive was to extend her relations of commerce in the new world and to acquire additional security for her possessions there by forming a connection with this country when detached from Great Britain. To ascribe to her any other motives—to suppose that she was actuated by friendship towards us or by a regard for our particular advantage—is to be ignorant of the springs of action which invariably regulate the cabinets of princes.

Relations with France, 1795-1796

National Obligations

❧ ❧

The established *rules of morality and justice are applicable to nations as well as to individuals*; that the *former* as well as the *latter* are bound *to keep their promises*, to *fulfil their engagements*, to *respect the rights of property* which others have acquired under contracts with them.

"The Vindication No. III,"
Philadelphia, May-August, 1792

Faith and justice between nations are virtues of a nature sacred and unequivocal. They cannot be too strongly inculcated nor too highly respected.

"Pacificus No. IV," Philadelphia,
July 10, 1793

Mutual charges of breach of faith are not uncommon between nations. Yet this does not prevent their making new stipulations with each other and relying upon their performance.

"The Defence No. VIII,"
New York, August 15, 1795

National Power

❧ ❧

'Tis as great an error for a nation to overrate as to underrate itself. Presumption is as great a fault as timidity.

To George Washington, Philadelphia,
April 14, 1794

National Pride

❧ ❧

National pride is generally a very intractable thing.

> "The Defence No. II," New York,
> July 25, 1795

National Safety

❧ ❧

The safety of a republic depends essentially on the energy of a common national sentiment; on a uniformity of principles and habits; on the exemption of the citizens from foreign bias and prejudice; and on that love of country which will almost invariably be found to be closely connected with birth, education, and family.

> "The Examination Number VIII,"
> New York, January 12, 1802

National Unity

❧ ❧

The safety of the whole depends upon the mutual protection of every part. If the sword of oppression be permitted to lop off one limb without opposition, reiterated strokes will soon dismember the whole body.

> *The Farmer Refuted*, New York,
> February 23, 1775

Political societies in close neighborhood must either be strongly united under one government or there will infallibly exist emulations and quarrels. This is in human nature; and we have no reason to think ourselves wiser or better than other men.

> To Elizabeth Hamilton, Light Camp,
> New York, August 16, 1781

Want of unanimity will naturally tend to render the operations of war feeble and heavy—to destroy both effort and perseverance. War undertaken under such auspices can scarcely end in anything better than an inglorious and disadvantageous peace. What worse it may produce is beyond the reach of human foresight.

> To George Washington, Philadelphia,
> April 14, 1794

Nations

❧

To defend its own rights, to vindicate its own honor, there are occasions when a nation ought to hazard even its existence.

> "Americanus No. II," Philadelphia,
> February 7, 1794

Reason, religion, philosophy, [and] policy disavow the spurious and odious doctrine that we ought to cherish and cultivate enmity with any nation whatever.

> "Horatius No. II," New York,
> July 1795

Native Americans

❧

It cannot be denied that frequent and great provocations to a spirit of animosity and revenge are given by them [Indians]; but a candid and impartial survey of the events which have from time to time occurred can leave no doubt that injuries and provocations have been too far mutual—that there is much to blame in the conduct of the frontier inhabitants as well as in that of the Indians. And the result of a full examination must be that unless means to restrain, by punishing the violences which those inhabitants are in the habit of perpetrating against the Indians, can be put in execution, all endeavors to preserve peace with them must be for ever frustrated.

To George Mathews, Philadelphia,
September 25, 1794

Natural Law

To grant that there is a supreme intelligence who rules the world and has established laws to regulate the actions of his creatures, and still to assert that man in a state of nature may be considered as perfectly free from all restraints of *law* and *government*, appears to a common understanding altogether irreconcilable.

The Farmer Refuted, New York, February 23, 1775

In a state of nature no man had any *moral* power to deprive another of his life, limbs, property, or liberty; nor the least authority to command or exact obedience from him, except that which arose from the ties of consanguinity.

The Farmer Refuted, New York, February 23, 1775

To usurp dominion over a people . . . , or to grasp at a more extensive power than they are willing to entrust, is to violate that law of nature which gives every man a right to his personal liberty and can, therefore, confer no obligation to obedience.

The Farmer Refuted, New York, February 23, 1775

When the first principles of civil society are violated and the rights of a whole people are invaded, the common forms of municipal law are not to be regarded. Men may then betake themselves to the law of nature; and if they but conform their actions to that standard, all cavils against them betray either ignorance or dishonesty.

The Farmer Refuted, New York,
February 23, 1775

A Navy

An active external commerce demands a naval power to protect it.

Draft of George Washington's Eighth Annual Address to
Congress, New York, November 10, 1796

Neutrality

The rights of neutrality will only be respected when they are defended by an adequate power. A nation, despicable by its weakness, forfeits even the privilege of being neutral.

The Federalist No. 11, New York,
November 24, 1787

Military expeditions out of the territory of a neutral power cannot rightfully be made by a power at war, and . . . if permitted, the neutral nation is answerable.

To William Lewis, Philadelphia, July 1793

It is a truth which our experience has confirmed that the most equitable and sincere neutrality is not sufficient to exempt a state from the depredations of other nations at war with each other.

Draft of George Washington's Eighth Annual Address to Congress, New York, November 10, 1796

North and South

❦ ❧

In the South it is supposed that more government than is expedient is desired by the North. In the North it is believed that the prejudices of the South are incompatible with the necessary degree of government and with the attainment of the essential ends of National Union.

To George Washington, Philadelphia, August 18, 1792

Opinion

❦ ❧

Opinion, whether well or ill founded, is the governing principle of human affairs.

To William Duer, Valley Forge, June 18, 1778

The manner in which a thing is done has more influence than is commonly imagined. Men are governed by opinion; this opinion is as much influenced by appearances as by realities; if a government appears to be confident of its own powers, it is the

surest way to inspire the same confidence in others; if it is diffi-
dent, it may be certain there will be a still greater diffidence in
others and that its authority will not only be distrusted [and]
controverted but contemned.

To James Duane, Liberty Pole, New Jersey, September 3, 1780

Opposition

❧ ☙

Men often oppose a thing merely because they have had no
agency in planning it or because it may have been planned by
those whom they dislike.

The Federalist No. 70, New York, March 15, 1788

Oppression

❧ ☙

The experience of past ages may inform us that when the circumstances of a people render them distressed, their rulers generally recur to severe, cruel, and oppressive measures. Instead of
endeavoring to establish their authority in the *affection* of their
subjects, they think they have no security but in their *fear*.

The Farmer Refuted, New York, February 23, 1775

Optimism

❧ ☙

It is a maxim of my life to enjoy the present good with the highest relish and to soften the present evil by a hope of future good.

To Elizabeth Schuyler, Bergen County,
New Jersey, July 6, 1780

Paper Money

❧ ❧

Past experience would forbid its being again successfully employed, and no friend to the morals, property, or industry of the people, [or] to public or private credit would desire to see it revived.

"Americanus No. I," Philadelphia,
January 31, 1794

Parental Feelings

❧ ❧

Alas, my Charmer, great are my fears—poignant my distress. I feel every day more and more how dear this Child is to me and I cease not to pray heaven for his recovery.

To Elizabeth Hamilton, Philadelphia,
August 2, 1794

The state of our dear sick angel continues too precarious. My heart trembles whenever I open a letter from you.

To Elizabeth Hamilton, Philadelphia,
August 17, 1794

Party Spirit

❧ ❧

Party spirit is an inseparable appendage of human nature. It grows naturally out of the rival passions of men and is therefore to be found in all governments. . . . This most dangerous spirit is apt to rage with greatest violence in governments of the popular kind and is at once their most common and their most fatal disease. Hence the disorders, convulsions, and tumults which have so often disturbed the repose, marred the happiness, and overturned the liberties of republics, enabling the leaders of the parties to become the masters and oppressors of the People.

"The Defence No. I," New York, July 22, 1795

'Tis to be lamented that already the spirit of party has made so great a progress in our infant republic. But it is at the same time a source of consolation that it as yet has its bounds—and that there are many who will only go a certain length in compliance with its dictates.

To William Short, Philadelphia,
March 15, 1793

Passions

It frequently happens that the excess of one selfish passion either defeats its own end or counteracts another.

"Publius Letter III," Poughkeepsie, New York,
November 16, 1778

[People are] governed more by passion and prejudice than by an enlightened sense of their own interests.

To —, Morristown, New Jersey,
December 1779-March 1780

Take mankind as they are, and what are they governed by? Their passions. . . . Our prevailing passions are ambition and interest; and it will ever be the duty of a wise government to avail itself of those passions in order to make them subservient to the public good, for these ever induce us to action.

Speech at Constitutional Convention,
Philadelphia, June 22, 1787

Patriotism

A dispassionate and virtuous citizen of the UStates will scorn to stand on any but purely *American* ground. It will be his study to render his feeling and affections neutral and impartial towards all foreign nations. His prayer will be for peace and that his country may be as much as possible kept out of the destructive vortex of foreign politics. To speak figuratively, he will regard his own country as a wife to whom he is bound to be exclusively faithful and affectionate, and he will watch with a jealous attention every propensity of his heart to wander towards a foreign country, which he will regard as a mistress that may pervert his fidelity and mar his happiness.

> For the *Gazette of the United States*,
> Philadelphia, March-April 1793

The true Patriot who never fears to sacrifice popularity to what he believes to be the cause of [public] good [cannot] hesitate to endeavor to unmask the error.

> "The Defence No. V," New York,
> August 5, 1795

The problem now to be solved is whether we will maintain or surrender our sovereignty. To maintain it with firmness is the most sacred of duties, the most glorious of tasks. The happiness of our country, the honor of the American name, demands it. The genius of Independence exhorts to it.

> "The Stand No. I," New York, March 30, 1798

'Tis not the triumph over a political rival which the true lover of his country desires; 'tis the safety, 'tis the welfare of that country, and he will gladly share with his bitterest opponent the glory of defending and preserving her.

> "The Stand No. VI," New York, April 19, 1798

It is the fervent wish of patriotism that our councils and nation may be united and resolute. The dearest interests call for it. A great public danger commands it.

"The Stand No. VI," New York,
April 19, 1798

Peace

❧ ❧

PEACE in the particular situation of this country is an object of such great and primary magnitude that it ought not to be relinquished unless the relinquishment be clearly necessary to PRESERVE OUR HONOR in some RIGHT or INTEREST of MATERIAL and PERMANENT importance.

"The Defence No. V," New York, August 5, 1795

Those which have strong motives to avoid war should by their moderation facilitate the accommodation of differences. This is a rule of good sense, a maxim of sound policy.

"The Defence No. V," New York, August 5, 1795

'Tis our true policy to remain at peace if we can, to negotiate our subjects of complaint as long as they shall be at all negotiable, to bear all that a free and independent people is at liberty to bear, to defer a resort to arms 'till a last effort of negotiation shall have demonstrated that there is no alternative but the surrender of our sovereignty or the defense of it, that the only option is between infamy or war.

"The Warning No. II," New York,
February 7, 1797

Peace Treaties

The common interests of humanity and the general tranquility of the world require that the power of making peace, wherever lodged, should be construed and exercised liberally; and even in cases where its extent may be doubtful, it is the policy of all wise nations to give it latitude rather than confine it.

Second Letter from Phocion,
New York, April 1784

'Tis the essence of a treaty of peace to extinguish all questions on that head and to secure to each party amnesty and indemnity. Without this the state of war would continue and would be inextinguishable.

"Philo Camillus No. 3," New York,
August 12, 1795

The People

The voice of the people has been said to be the voice of God; and however generally this maxim has been quoted and believed, it is not true in fact. The people are turbulent and changing; they seldom judge or determine right.

Speech at Constitutional Convention,
Philadelphia, June 18, 1787

The fabric of American Empire ought to rest on the solid basis of THE CONSENT OF THE PEOPLE. The streams of national power ought to flow immediately from that pure original fountain of all legitimate authority.

The Federalist No. 22, New York, December 14, 1787

Perceptions

A degree of illusion mixes itself in all the affairs of society. The opinion of objects has more influence than their real nature.

To —, Morristown, New Jersey,
December 1779-March 1780

In a popular government *appearances* are a good deal.

To Jonathan Dayton, New York,
March 30, 1798

Perjury

Perjury is, no doubt, a most heinous and detestable crime, and for my part, I had rather suffer anything than have my wants relieved at the expense of truth and integrity.

A Full Vindication of the Measures of Congress,
New York, December 15, 1774

Persecution

In politics as in religion it is equally absurd to aim at making proselytes by fire and sword. Heresies in either can rarely be cured by persecution.

The Federalist No. 1, New York,
October 27, 1787

Personal Attacks

❦

Such is my opinion of your abilities as a critic that I very much prefer your disapprobation to your applause.

The Farmer Refuted, New York,
February 23, 1775

'Tis not the load of proper official business that alone engrosses me, though this would be enough to occupy any man. 'Tis not the extra attentions I am obliged to pay to the course of legislative maneuvers that alone add to my burthen and perplexity. 'Tis the malicious intrigues to stab me in the dark, against which I am too often obliged to guard myself, that distract and harass me to a point which, rendering my situation scarcely tolerable, interferes with objects to which friendship and inclination would prompt me.

To John Jay, Philadelphia,
December 18, 1792

I console myself with these lines of the poet:

He needs must have of optics keen
Who sees what is not to be seen—
And with this belief that in spite of calumny,
The friends I love and esteem will continue to love and esteem me.

To Catharine Greene, Philadelphia,
September 3, 1793

Never was there a more ungenerous persecution of any man than of myself. Not only the worst constructions are put upon my conduct as a public man, but it seems my birth is the subject of the most humiliating criticism.

To William Jackson, New York,
August 26, 1800

Poetry

Not being a poet myself, I am in the less danger of feeling mortification at the idea that in the career of dramatic composition at least female genius in the United States has outstripped the male.

To Mercy Otis Warren,
Philadelphia, July 1, 1791

Political Change

Vibrations of power, you are aware, are . . . the genius of our government.

To Rufus King, New York,
June 3, 1802

Political Creed

As to my own political creed, I give it to you with the utmost sincerity. I am *affectionately* attached to the republican theory. I desire *above all things* to see the *equality* of political rights exclusive of all *hereditary* distinction firmly established by a practical demonstration of its being consistent with the order and happiness of society.

To Edward Carrington,
Philadelphia, May 26, 1792

Political Opposition

🌿 🌿

Every new political occurrence renders it more and more apparent that there is a description of men in this country continually on the watch to defame and, if possible, to convulse the government of the Ustates. No important measure of that government from whatever quarter it proceeds can escape their malevolent vigilance.

On the Rise of a War Party,
Philadelphia, 1793

Political Parties

🌿 🌿

'Tis curious to observe the anticipations of the different parties. One side appears to believe that there is a serious plot to overturn the state governments and substitute monarchy [for] the present republican system. The other side firmly believes that there is a serious plot to overturn the General Government and elevate the separate power of the states upon its ruins. Both sides may be equally wrong, and their mutual jealousies may be materially causes of the appearances which mutually disturb them and sharpen them against each other.

To George Washington, Philadelphia,
August 18, 1792

The spirit of party has grown to maturity sooner in this country than perhaps was to have been counted upon.

To William Short, Philadelphia,
February 5, 1793

There is an opinion that parties in free countries are salutary checks upon the administration of the government and serve to keep alive the spirit of liberty. This within certain bounds is probably true, and in governments of a monarchical cast, patriotism may look with indulgence on the spirit of party. But in governments of the popular character, in those purely elective, it is a spirit not to be fostered.

Draft of George Washington's Farewell Address,
New York, August 10, 1796

Political Power

The public business must in some way or other go forward. If a pertinacious minority can control the opinion of a majority respecting the best mode of conducting it, the majority in order that something may be done must conform to the views of the minority; and thus the sense of the smaller number will over-rule that of the greater and give a tone to the national proceedings.

The Federalist No. 22, New York,
December 14, 1787

Political Realities

The triumphs of vice are no new things under the sun. And I fear 'till the millennium comes, in spite of all our boasted light and purification, hypocrisy and treachery will continue to be the most successful commodities in the political market. It seems to be the destined lot of nations to mistake their foes for their friends, their flatterers for their faithful servants.

To Richard Harison, Philadelphia,
January 5, 1793

Politics

❧ ☙

The contest between us is indeed a war of principles—a war between tyranny and liberty, but not between monarchy and republicanism.

An Address to the Electors of the State of New-York,
March 21, 1801

I am far from thinking that a man is bound to quit a public office merely because the administration of the government may have changed hands. But when those who have come into power are undisguised persecutors of the party to which he has been attached and study with ostentation to heap upon it every indignity and injury, he ought not in my opinion to permit himself to be made an except[ion] or to lend his talents to the support of such characters.

To Rufus King, New York,
June 3, 1802

Popular Assemblies

❧ ☙

Are not popular assemblies frequently subject to the impulses of rage, resentment, jealousy, avarice, and of other irregular and violent propensities? Is it not well known that their determinations are often governed by a few individuals in whom they place confidence and are of course liable to be tinctured by the passions and views of those individuals?

The Federalist No. 6, New York,
November 14, 1787

Popular Government

❧ ❧

The situation of the state with respect to its internal government is not more pleasing. Here we find the general disease which infects all our constitutions, an excess of popularity. There is no *order* that has a will of its own. The inquiry constantly is what will *please*, not what will *benefit*, the people. In such a government there can be nothing but temporary expedient, fickleness, and folly.

To Robert Morris, Albany, New York, August 13, 1782

'Tis essentially true that virtue or morality is a main and necessary spring of popular or republican governments. The rule indeed extends with more or less force to all free governments.

Draft of George Washington's Farewell Address,
New York, July 30, 1796

Every day shows more and more the much to be regretted tendency of governments entirely popular to dissolution and disorder.

Speech at Meeting of Federalists, Albany,
New York, February 10, 1804

Power

❧ ❧

A fondness for power is implanted in most men, and it is natural to abuse it when acquired. This maxim, drawn from the experience of all ages, makes it the height of folly to entrust any set of men with power which is not under every possible control.

The Farmer Refuted, New York,
February 23, 1775

As too much power leads to despotism, too little leads to anarchy, and both eventually to the ruin of the people.

> "The Continentalist No. 1," Fishkill,
> New York, July 12, 1781

The possibility of a power being abused is no argument against its existence.

> Speech in New York Assembly, New York, January 19, 1787

Men love power.

> Speech at Constitutional Convention,
> Philadelphia, June 18, 1787

There is in the nature of sovereign power an impatience of control that disposes those who are invested with the exercise of it to look with an evil eye upon all external attempts to restrain or direct its operations.

> *The Federalist No. 15*, New York,
> December 1, 1787

It is not for the friends of good government to employ extraordinary expedients which ought only to be resorted to in cases of great magnitude and urgent necessity.

> To Rufus King, Philadelphia,
> July 25, 1792

The Practice of Law

I have been employed for the last ten months in . . . studying the art of fleecing my neighbors.

> To Marquis de Lafayette, Albany,
> New York, November 3, 1782

You are condemned to run the race of ambition all your life. I am already tired of the career and dare to leave it.

To Marquis de Lafayette, Albany,
New York, November 3, 1782

Precedents

Bad precedents influence as well as good. They are greedily looked up to and cited by men of loose principles who make them instruments of instilling doctrines and feelings hostile to morals, property, and credit.

The Defence of the Funding System,
New York, July 1795

The Presidency

Energy in the executive is a leading character in the definition of good government. It is essential to the protection of the community against foreign attacks. It is not less essential to the steady administration of the laws, to the protection of property against those irregular and high handed combinations which sometimes interrupt the ordinary course of justice, [and] to the security of liberty against the enterprises and assaults of ambition, of faction and of anarchy.

The Federalist No. 70, New York,
March 15, 1788

The public good requires as a primary object that the dignity of the office should be supported. Whatever is essential to this ought to be pursued though at the risk of partial or momentary dissatisfaction.

To George Washington, New York, May 5, 1789

Presidential Power

There is no part of his functions in which it is upon principle more essential that the Executive should be perfectly free from extrinsic influence of every kind than that of the choice of officers.

Circular to the Commandants of Regiments,
New York, May 23, 1799

The Press

The liberty of the press consists in my idea in publishing the truth from good motives and for justifiable ends, though it reflect [badly] on government, on magistrates, or individuals. If it be not allowed, it excludes the privilege of canvassing men and our rulers.

Speech in *People v. Croswell*, Albany,
New York, February 14-15, 1804

Principles

It is perhaps always better that partial evils should be submitted to than that principles should be violated.

To George Washington, Philadelphia,
May 28, 1790

Promises

The promises of princes and statesmen are of little weight. They never bind longer than 'till a strong temptation offers to break them; and they are frequently made with a sinister design.

The Farmer Refuted, New York,
February 23, 1775

A promise must never be broken; and I never will make you one which I will not fulfil as far as I am able.

To Philip A. Hamilton, Philadelphia,
December 5, 1791

How deplorable will it be, should it ever become proverbial that a President of the United States, like the *weird sisters* in Macbeth, *"Keeps his promise to the ear, but breaks it to the sense!"*

"The Examination Number IV," New York,
December 26, 1801

Promotion

The expectation of promotion in civil as in military life is a great stimulus to virtuous exertion.

To George Washington,
Philadelphia, April 17, 1791

Property Rights

❧ ❧

Wherever indeed a right of property is infringed for the general good, if the nature of the case admits of compensation, it ought to be made.

> "The Vindication No. III," Philadelphia,
> May-August 1792

Public Credit

❧ ❧

Public credit [is] the palladium of public safety.

> To George Washington, Philadelphia,
> August 18, 1792

There can be no time, no state of things, in which credit is not essential to a nation, especially as long as nations in general continue to use it as a resource in war.

> *Report on Public Credit*, Philadelphia,
> January 16, 1795

War without credit would be more than a great calamity—[it] would be ruin.

> *Report on Public Credit*, Philadelphia,
> January 16, 1795

Public and private credit are closely allied if not inseparable. There is perhaps no example of the one being in a flourishing [state] where the other was in a bad state.

> *Report on Public Credit*, Philadelphia,
> January 16, 1795

Cherish public credit as a means of strength and security. As one method of preserving it, use it as little as possible.

Draft of George Washington's Farewell Address,
New York, July 30, 1796

Public Debt

❧ ☙

Public debt has been truly defined *"A property subsisting in the faith of Government."* Its essence is promise.

"The Defence No. XIX," New York,
October 14, 1795

The Public Good

❧ ☙

We ought not to sacrifice the public good to narrow scruples.

Speech at Constitutional Convention,
Philadelphia, June 18, 1787

Public Office

❧ ☙

Public Office in this country has few attractions. The pecuniary emolument is so inconsiderable as to amount to a sacrifice to any man who can employ his time with advantage in any liberal profession. The opportunity of doing good, from the jealousy of power and the spirit of faction, is too small in any station to warrant a long continuance of private sacrifices.

To William Hamilton, Albany,
New York, May 2, 1797

Public Officials

But you remember the saying with regard to Caesar's wife. I think the spirit of it applicable to every man concerned in the administration of the finances of a country.

To Henry Lee, New York,
December 1, 1789

Public Opinion

In popular governments the sentiments of the people generally take their tone from their leaders.

Speech in New York Assembly,
New York, March 28, 1787

Public infamy must restrain what the laws cannot.

To Philip Livingston, Philadelphia,
April 2, 1792

Public Pay

True economy, as applied to a nation, does not consist in the penurious apportionment of the compensations of its officers, but in the steady adherence to an enlightened and comprehensive system, which, among other effects, placing the management of its affairs in able and faithful hands, causes all its great pecuniary operations to be conducted both with skill and integrity.

Report on Petition of William Gardner,
Philadelphia, January 31, 1795

Public Service

❦

I would not be fool enough to make pecuniary sacrifices and endure a life of extreme drudgery without opportunity either to do material good or to acquire reputation.

To Edward Carrington, Philadelphia, May 26, 1792

Public Speaking

❦

It is a common practice in entering upon the discussion of an important subject to endeavor to conciliate the good-will of the audience to the speaker by professions of disinterestedness and zeal for the public good.

Speech in New York Assembly,
New York, February 15, 1787

Punishment

❦

The efficacy of punishment, when requisite, depends much upon its celerity.

To James McHenry, Philadelphia, December 1799

Reform

❧

The first step to reformation . . . is to be sensible of our faults.

To Marquis de Barbe-Marbois, New Windsor,
New York, February 7, 1781

Religion and Morality

❧

To all those dispositions which promote political prosperity, religion and morality are essential props.

To George Washington,
New York, July 30, 1796

Religious Enthusiasm

❧

Enthusiasm is certainly a very good thing, but religious enthusiasm is at least a dangerous instrument.

To William S. Smith, New York,
March 12, 1800

Religious Fanaticism

❧

The world has been scourged with many fanatical sects in religion, who, inflamed by a sincere but mistaken zeal, have perpet-
uated under the idea of serving God the most atrocious crimes.

The Cause of France,
Philadelphia, 1794

Republics

❧ ☙

Have republics in practice been less addicted to war than monarchies? Are not the former administered by *men* as well as the latter? Are there not aversions, predilections, rivalships, and desires of unjust acquisition that affect nations as well as kings?

The Federalist No. 6, New York, November 14, 1787

One of the weak sides of republics, among their numerous advantages, is that they afford too easy an inlet to foreign corruption.

The Federalist No. 22, New York,
December 14, 1787

The truth seems to be that all governments have been deemed republics in which a large portion of the sovereignty has been vested in the whole or in a considerable body of the people; and that none have been deemed monarchies, as contrasted with the republican standard, in which there has not been an *hereditary* chief magistrate.

To the *New York Evening Post*, New York, February 24, 1802

Respect Abroad

❧ ☙

In proportion as the estimation of our resources is exalted in the eyes of foreign nations, the respect for us must increase; and this must beget a proportionable caution neither to insult nor injure us with levity.

Report on Public Credit, Philadelphia,
December 13, 1790

Revolution

❧ ❧

An extreme jealousy of power is the attendant on all popular revolutions and has seldom been without its evils. It is to this source we are to trace many of the fatal mistakes which have so deeply endangered the common cause.

> "The Continentalist No. I," Fishkill,
> New York, July 12, 1781

In those great revolutions which occasionally convulse society, human nature never fails to be brought forward in its brightest as well as in its blackest colors. And it has very properly been ranked not among the least of the advantages which compensate for the evils they produce that they serve to bring to light talents and virtues which might otherwise have languished in obscurity or only shot forth a few scattered and wandering rays.

> Eulogy on Nathanael Greene,
> New York, July 4, 1789

It is not justifiable in any government or nation to hold out to the world a *general invitation* and *encouragement* to *revolution* and insurrection under a promise of *fraternity* and *assistance*. Such a step is of a nature to disturb the repose of mankind, to excite fermentation in every country, to endanger government everywhere. Nor can there be a doubt that wheresoever a spirit of this kind appears, it is lawful to repress and repel it.

> To George Washington, Philadelphia,
> May 2, 1793

The passions of a revolution are apt to hurry even good men into excesses.

> "Philo Camillus No. 3," New York,
> August 12, 1795

The Revolutionary War Debt

※ ✣

It was the price of liberty.

Report on Public Credit, New York, January 9, 1790

Maria Reynolds

※ ✣

The variety of shapes which this woman could assume was endless.

Observations on Certain Documents,
New York, August 25, 1797

Rights

※ ✣

The sacred rights of mankind are not to be rummaged for among old parchments or musty records. They are written, as with a sunbeam, in the whole *volume* of human nature by the hand of the divinity itself and can never be erased or obscured by mortal power.

The Farmer Refuted, New York, February 23, 1775

The rights of government are as essential to be defended as the rights of individuals.

To John Dickinson, Albany, New York,
September 25-30, 1783

Rome

Rome was the nurse of freedom. She was celebrated for her justice and lenity; but in what manner did she govern her dependent provinces? They were made the continual scene of rapine and cruelty. From thence let us learn how little confidence is due to the wisdom and equity of the most exemplary nations.

A Full Vindication of the Measures of Congress,
New York, December 15, 1774

Rules

All general rules are to be construed with certain reasonable limitations.

To George Washington, Philadelphia, May 2, 1793

Sacrifice

Great sacrifices ought to be made for a great object, but to make them or hazard them for an inferior object would be folly in the extreme.

To the Citizens of the City of New York,
New York, April 22, 1796

My public labors have amounted to an absolute sacrifice of the interests of my family.

Explanation of Financial Situation,
New York, July 1, 1804

Seamen

❧ ❧

Seamen [are] that sinew of maritime power.

"The Warning No. IV," New York,
February 27, 1797

Selfishness

❧ ❧

A vast majority of mankind is entirely biased by motives of self-interest. Most men are glad to remove any burdens off themselves and place them upon the necks of their neighbors.

A Full Vindication of the Measures of Congress,
New York, December 15, 1774

It is the temper of societies as well as of individuals to be impatient of constraint and to prefer partial [i.e., their own] to general interest.

"The Continentalist No. II," Fishkill,
New York, July 19, 1781

Self-Preservation

❧ ❧

Self preservation is the first principle of our nature. When our lives and properties are at stake, it would be foolish and unnatural to refrain from such measures as might preserve them because they would be detrimental to others.

A Full Vindication of the Measures of Congress,
New York, December 15, 1774

Self-Protection

Whenever a particular nation adopts maxims of conduct contrary to [th]ose generally established among nations [and] calculated to disturb their tranquillity and to expose their safety, they may justifiably make a common cause to oppose and control such nation.

"Pacificus No. II," Philadelphia,
July 3, 1793

Separation of Powers

It is a fundamental maxim of free government, that the three great departments of power, *Legislative*, *Executive* and *Judiciary*, shall be essentially distinct and independent the one of the other.

"The Examination Number XIV,"
New York, March 2, 1802

Slander

It is well known that I have long been the object of the most malignant calumnies of the faction opposed to our government through the medium of the papers devoted to their views.

To Josiah Ogden Hoffman, New York,
November 6, 1799

I consider this spirit of abuse and calumny as the pest of society. I know the best of men are not exempt from the attacks of slander. . . . Drops of water, in long and continued succession, will wear out adamant.

Speech in *People v. Croswell*, Albany, New York,
February 14-15, 1804

Slavery

❦

The only distinction between freedom and slavery consists in this: In the former state, a man is governed by the laws to which he has given his consent, either in person or by his representative. In the latter, he is governed by the will of another. In the one case his life and property are his own, in the other they depend upon the pleasure of a master. It is easy to discern which of these two states is preferable. No man in his senses can hesitate in choosing to be free rather than a slave.

A Full Vindication of the Measures of Congress,
New York, December 15, 1774

Were not the disadvantages of slavery too obvious to stand in need of it, I might enumerate and describe the tedious train of calamities inseparable from it. I might show that it is fatal to religion and morality; that it tends to debase the mind and corrupt its noblest springs of action. I might show that it relaxes the sinews of industry, clips the wings of commerce, and introduces misery and indigence in every shape.

A Full Vindication of the Measures of Congress,
New York, December 15, 1774

The laws of certain states which give an ownership in the service of negroes as personal property constitute a similitude between them and other articles of personal property and thereby subject them to the right of capture by war. But being men, by the laws

141

of God and nature they were capable of acquiring liberty, and when the captor in war, to whom by the capture the ownership was transferred, thought fit to give the liberty, the gift was not only valid but irrevocable.

"Philo Camillus No. 2," New York, August 7, 1795

Slow but Sure

❧ ❧

Slow and sure is not [a] bad maxim. Snails are a wise generation.

To Theodore Sedgwick, New York, February 27, 1800

Social Standing

❧ ❧

The changes in the human conditions are uncertain and frequent. Many on whom fortune has bestowed her favors may trace their family to a more unprosperous station; and many who are now in obscurity may look back upon the affluence and exalted rank of their ancestors.

Speech at New York Ratifying Convention,
Poughkeepsie, New York, June 28, 1788

Soldiers

❧ ❧

It is a maxim with some great military judges that with sensible officers soldiers can hardly be too stupid.

To John Jay, Middlebrook, New Jersey, March 14, 1779

Sovereignty

❧ ☙

The jurisdiction of every *Independent Nation*, within its own territories, naturally excludes all exercise of authority by any other government within those territories unless by its own consent or in consequence of stipulations in treaties. Every such exercise of authority therefore not warranted by consent or treaty is an intrusion on the jurisdiction of the country within which it is exercised and amounts to an injury and affront, more or less great, according to the nature of the case.

> To George Washington, Philadelphia,
> May 15, 1793

Statesmen

❧ ☙

Statesmen are but men and far more actuated by their passions than they ought to be.

> To Henry Lee, Philadelphia,
> June 22, 1793

Statesmanship

❧ ☙

No wise statesman will reject the good from an apprehension of the ill. The truth is in human affairs there is no good, pure and unmixed; every advantage has two sides, and wisdom consists in availing ourselves of the good and guarding as much as possible against the bad.

> To Robert Morris, De Peyster's Point,
> New York, April 30, 1781

Is it a recommendation to have *no theory?* Can that man be a systematic or able statesman who has none? I believe not.

To James A. Bayard, New York, January 16, 1801

States Rights

❧ ⚘

This is the first symptom of a spirit which must either be killed or will kill the Constitution of the United States.

To John Jay, Philadelphia, November 13, 1790

Subversion of Government

❧ ⚘

The only enemy which republicanism has to fear in this country is in the spirit of faction and anarchy. If this will not permit the ends of government to be attained under it, if it engenders disorders in the community, all regular and orderly minds will wish for a change, and the demagogues who have produced the disorder will make it for their own aggrandizement. This is the old story.

To Edward Carrington, Philadelphia, May 26, 1792

Every republic at all times has it Catalines and its Caesars. Men of this stamp, while in their hearts they scoff at the principles of liberty, while in their real characters they are arbitrary, persecuting, intolerant, and despotic, are in all their harangues and professions the most zealous, nay, if they are to be believed, the only friends to liberty.

"The Vindication No. I," Philadelphia,
May-August 1792

Supply and Demand

❧ ☙

Price naturally keeps pace with competition and demand; whatever increases the latter, necessarily tends to an augmentation of the former.

Report on Public Loans, Philadelphia, February 13-14, 1793

Sycophancy

❧ ☙

In courts, sycophants flatter the errors and prejudices of the prince; in republics sycophants flatter the errors and prejudices of the people. In both, honest and independent men are frequently obliged to tell unpalatable truths, which are well or ill received according to the virtue and good sense of those to whom they are addressed.

"Philo Camillus No. 3," New York, August 12, 1795

Taxes

❧ ☙

This you may depend upon, if ever you let the Parliament carry its point, you will have these [taxes] and more to pay. Perhaps before long, your tables and chairs, and platters and dishes, and knives and forks, and everything else would be taxed. Nay, I don't know but they would find means to tax you for every child you got, and for every kiss your daughters received from their sweethearts, and, God knows, that would soon ruin you.

A Full Vindication of the Measures of Congress,
New York, December 15, 1774

The great art is to distribute the public burdens well and not suffer them, either first or last, to fall too heavily upon parts of the community; else distress and disorder must ensue.

"The Continentalist No. VI,"
Fishkill, New York,
July 4, 1782

The genius of liberty reprobates everything arbitrary or discretionary in taxation. It exacts that every man by a definite and general rule should know what proportion of his property the state demands.

"The Continentalist No. VI,"
Fishkill, New York,
July 4, 1782

Do we imagine that our assessments operate equally? Nothing can be more contrary to the fact. Wherever a discretionary power is lodged in any set of men over the property of their neighbors, they will abuse it.

"The Continentalist No. VI,"
Fishkill, New York,
July 4, 1782

Equality and certainty are the two great objects to be aimed at in taxation.

Speech in New York Assembly,
New York, February 17, 1787

Happy it is when the interest which the government has in the preservation of its own power coincides with a proper distribution of the public burdens and tends to guard the least wealthy part of the community from oppression!

The Federalist No. 36, New York,
January 8, 1788

Taxes are never welcome to a community. They seldom fail to excite uneasy sensations more or less extensive. Hence a too strong propensity [exists] in the governments of nations to anticipate and mortgage the resources of posterity rather than encounter the inconveniences of a present increase of taxes. But this policy, when not dictated by very peculiar circumstances, is of the worst kind. Its obvious tendency is, by enhancing the permanent burdens of the people, to produce lasting distress, and its natural issue is in national bankruptcy.

Report on Additional Supplies,
Philadelphia, March 16, 1792

It is true the merchants have complained [of recent taxes], but so they did of the first impost law for a time, and so men always will do at an augmentation of taxes which touch the business they carry on, especially in a country where no or scarcely any *such* taxes before existed.

To George Washington, Philadelphia,
August 18, 1782

It is a good rule of caution that no more of the public revenues should be rendered permanent than is necessary to give moral certainty to the provisions which may be regarded as the pillars of public credit.

Report on Public Credit, Philadelphia,
January 16, 1795

The ignorant may not see the tax in the enhanced price of the commodity, but the man of reflection knows it is there.

Statement in *Hylton v.
United States* [ca. 1796]

As to *taxes*, they are evidently inseparable from government. It is impossible without them to pay the debts of the nation, to protect it from foreign danger, or to secure individuals from lawless violence and rapine.

*An Address to the Electors of the State
of New-York*, March 21, 1801

Tories

❦

That they are enemies of the natural rights of mankind is manifest because they wish to see one part of their species enslaved by another. That they have an invincible aversion to common sense is apparent in many respects. They endeavor to persuade us that the absolute sovereignty of Parliament does not imply our absolute slavery; that it is a Christian duty to submit to be plundered of all we have merely because some of our fellow subjects are wicked enough to require it of us, that slavery so far from being a great evil is a great blessing.

A Full Vindication of the Measures of Congress,
New York, December 15, 1774

Trade

❦

There are some who maintain that trade will regulate itself and is not to be benefitted by the encouragements or restraints of government. Such persons will imagine that there is no need of a common directing power. This is one of those wild speculative paradoxes which have grown into credit among us contrary to the uniform practice and sense of the most enlightened nations.

"The Continentalist No. V,"
Fishkill, New York,
April 18, 1782

To preserve the balance of trade in favor of a nation ought to be a leading aim of its policy.

"The Continentalist No. V,"
Fishkill, New York,
April 18, 1782

My commercial system turns very much on giving a free course to trade and cultivating good humor with all the world.

To Thomas Jefferson, Philadelphia, January 13, 1791

Proximity of territory invites to trade; the bordering inhabitants in spite of every prohibition will endeavor to carry it on; if not allowed, illicit adventures take place of the regular operations of legalized commerce.

"The Defence No. X," New York, August 26, 1795

Commerce, it is manifest, like any other object of enterprise or industry, will prosper in proportion as it is secure.

"The Defence No. XXI," New York, October 30, 1795

Treaties

Laws are the acts of legislation of a particular nation for itself. Treaties are the acts of the legislation of several nations for themselves jointly and reciprocally.

"The Defence No. XXXVI," New York, January 2, 1796

A treaty must necessarily repeal an antecedent law contrary to it; according to the legal maxim that *"leges posteriores priores contrarias abrogant"* [Posterior laws abrogate those which are prior to them if contradictory].

"The Defence No. XXXVII," New York, January 6, 1796

When one party to a treaty violates the compact in any material article, the other party is free to annul the whole.

To John Marshall, New York, October 2, 1800

Treatment of Employees

❧ ❧

It will have a bad effect to let the persons employed suffer.

To Benjamin Walker, Philadelphia, July 23, 1792

Trust

❧ ❧

I hold nothing so unsafe in public affairs as half confidence; that in my opinion to employ a man in delicate and important stations and to act towards him so as to convince him that he is not trusted and is not to receive the common share of public reward is the most effectual way that can be adopted to make him unfaithful.

To John Adams, New York,
September 7, 1799

Truth

❧ ❧

I love to speak the truth. . . . 'Tis my maxim to let the plain naked truth speak for itself; and if men won't listen to it, 'tis their own fault; they must be contented to suffer for it.

A Full Vindication of the Measures of Congress,
New York, December 15, 1774

The best way of determining disputes and of investigating truth is by descending to elementary principles. Any other method may only bewilder and misguide the understanding.

The Farmer Refuted, New York, February 23, 1775

Tyranny

❧

Give all power to the many, they will oppress the few. Give all power to the few, they will oppress the many. Both therefore ought to have power that each may defend itself against the other.

Speech at Constitutional Convention,
Philadelphia, June 18, 1787

The United States

❧

There is something noble and magnificent in the perspective of a great Federal Republic, closely linked in the pursuit of a common interest, tranquil and prosperous at home, respectable abroad.

"The Continentalist No. VI," Fishkill,
New York, July 4, 1782

We are a young and a growing Empire, with much enterprise and vigor, but undoubtedly are, and must be for years, rather an agricultural, than a manufacturing, people.

Conversation with George Beckwith,
New York, October 1789

The UStates, rooted as are now the ideas of independence, are happily too remote from Europe to be governed by her. Dominion over any part of them would be a real misfortune to any nation of that quarter of the globe.

"Americanus No. II," Philadelphia,
February 7, 1794

I observe more and more that by the jealousy and envy of some, the miserliness of others, and the concurring influence of *all foreign powers*, America, if she attains to greatness, must *creep* to it.

To Theodore Sedgwick, New York, February 27, 1800

As to the Country, it is too young and vigorous to be quacked out of its political health.

To Henry Lee, New York, March 7, 1800

Vanity

With some men, the hardest thing to forgive is the demonstration of their errors—the manifestation that they are not infallible. Mortified vanity is one of the most corroding emotions of the human mind, one of the most inextinguishable sources of animosity and hatred.

"The Vindication No. I," Philadelphia,
May-August 1792

Violence

When the sword is once drawn, the passions of men observe no bounds of moderation.

The Federalist No. 16, New York, December 4, 1787

Violent and unjust measures commonly defeat their own purpose.

"The Warning No. II," New York, February 7, 1797

Virtue

❧

There is no virtue [in] America. That commerce which pre-
side[d] [over] the birth and education of these states has [fitted]
their inhabitants for the chain, and . . . the only condition they
sincerely desire is that it may be a golden one.

> To John Laurens, West Point, New York,
> September 11, 1779

One of the strongest incentives to public virtue [is] the expectation of public esteem.

> Defense of the President's
> Neutrality Proclamation,
> Philadelphia, May 1793

Voting

❧

A share in the sovereignty of the state which is exercised by the
citizens at large in voting at elections is one of the most important rights of the subject and in a republic ought to stand fore-
most in the estimation of the law.

> *Second Letter from Phocion,*
> New York, April 1784

War

❧

The authorised maxims and practices of war are the satire of
human nature. They countenance almost every species of

seduction as well as violence; and the general that can make most traitors in the army of his adversary is frequently most applauded.

To John Laurens, Preakness, New Jersey,
October 11, 1780

We ought to recollect that in war to defend or attack are very different things; to the first, the mountains, the wildernesses, the militia, sometimes even the poverty of a country, will suffice; the latter requires an *army* and a *treasury*.

Speech in New York Assembly,
New York, March 28, 1787

War, like most other things, is a science to be acquired and perfected by diligence, by perseverance, by time, and by practice.

The Federalist No. 25, New York,
December 21, 1787

The fiery and destructive passions of war reign in the human breast with much more powerful sway than the mild and beneficent sentiments of peace.

The Federalist No. 34, New York, January 5, 1788

If the government is forced into a war, the cheerful support of the people may be counted upon. If it brings it upon itself, it will have to struggle with their displeasure and reluctance. This difference alone is immense!

To George Washington, New York,
September 15, 1790

Whenever a nation adopts maxims of conduct tending to the disturbance of the tranquillity and established order of its neighbors or manifesting a spirit of self-aggrandizement, it is lawful for other nations to combine against it and, by force, to control the effects of those maxims and that spirit.

To George Washington, Philadelphia, May 2, 1793

Wars oftener proceed from angry and perverse passions than from cool calculations of interest.

To George Washington, Philadelphia, April 14, 1794

The true inference is that we ought not lightly to seek or provoke a resort to arms; that in the differences between us and other nations we ought carefully to avoid measures which tend to widen the breach; and that we should sc[r]upulously abstain from whatever may be construed into reprisals 'till after the fruitless employment of all amicable means has reduced it to a certainty that there is no alternative.

"The Defence No. II," New York,
July 25, 1795

If there be a foreign power which sees with envy or ill will our growing prosperity, that power must discern that our infancy is the time for clipping our wings. We ought to be wise enough to see that this is not the time for trying our strength.

"The Defence No. II," New York,
July 25, 1795

Reason and experience teach that the great mass of expense in every country proceeds from war.

The Defence of the Funding System,
New York, July 1795

Our experience has already belied the reveries of those dreamers or imposters who were wont to [promise] to this country a perpetual exemption from war.

The Defence of the Funding System,
New York, July 1795

War in the modern system of it offers but two options: credit or the devastation of private property.

The Defence of the Funding System,
New York, July 1795

The seeds of war are sown thickly in the human breast.

> The Defence of the Funding System, New York, July 1795

There is no juncture at which war is more unwelcome to a nation than immediately after the experience of another war which has required great exertions and has been expensive, bloody, and calamitous.

> "The Defence No. VIII," New York,
> August 15, 1795

If one party could not convince the other by argument of the superior solidity of its pretensions, I know of no alternative, but ARBITRATION or WAR.

> "The Defence No. XIII," New York, September 5, 1795

Of all uncertain things, the issues of war are the most uncertain.

> "The Defence No. XIII," New York, September 5, 1795

When as in our late Revolution, the question was *Slavery* or *War*, 'twas our duty to forget every other consideration and to put everything to the hazard of the die; but when the question is to plunge into war to avenge partial injuries which do not threaten either our independence or our liberty, wisdom advises as to a very different course.

> To the Citizens of the City of New York,
> New York, April 22, 1796

War of itself gives to the parties a mutual right to kill in battle and to capture the persons and property of each other.

> "The Examination Number I," New York, December 17, 1801

War is offensive on the part of the state which makes it; on the opposite side, it is defensive; but the rights of both as to the measure of hostility are equal.

> "The Examination Number I," New York, December 17, 1801

War and Commerce

❧ ❧

The desire of a power at war to destroy the commerce of its enemy is a natural effect of the state of war.

"The Warning No. I," New York, January 27, 1797

War and Peace

❧ ❧

Let us recollect that peace or war will not always be left to our option; that however moderate or unambitious we may be, we cannot count upon the moderation, or hope to extinguish the ambition, of others.

The Federalist No. 34, New York, January 5, 1788

War Preparations

❧ ❧

Being prepared for war [is] one of the best securities to our peace.

Draft of a Proposed Message from George Washington to Congress, Philadelphia, March-May 1794

When one nation inflicts injuries upon another which are causes of war . . . the usual and received course is to prepare for war and proceed to negotiation. . . . Preparations for war in such cases contains in it nothing offensive. It is a mere precaution for self defense under circumstances which endanger the breaking out of war.

To George Washington, Philadelphia, April 14, 1794

The preparation against danger by timely and provident disbursements is often a means of avoiding greater disbursements to repel it.

> Draft of George Washington's Farewell Address,
> New York, July 30, 1796

We shall best guarantee ourselves against calamity by preparing for the worst.

> To Timothy Pickering, New York,
> March 22, 1797

To have a good army on foot will be best of all precautions to prevent as well as to repel invasion.

> "The Stand No. VI," New York,
> April 19, 1798

Absurd indeed must be that American who will rest the safety of his country on any other foundation than her own ability to repel violence.

> To John Marshall, New York, October 2, 1800

War Stories

❧

To embellish military exploits and varnish military disgraces is no unusual policy.

> "H. G. Letter II," New York, February 21, 1789

George Washington

❧

[George Washington was] that man who at the head of our armies fought so successfully for the liberty and independence which are now our pride and our boast; who during the war supported the hopes, united the hearts, and nerved the arm of his countrymen; who at the close of it, unseduced by ambition and the love of power, soothed and appeased the discontents of his suffering companions in arms and with them left the proud scenes of a victorious field for the modest retreats of private life.

> Defense of the President's Neutrality Proclamation,
> Philadelphia, May 1793

Perhaps no man in this community has equal cause with myself to deplore the loss. I have been much indebted to the kindness of the General, and he was an Aegis very essential to me.

> To Tobias Lear, New York,
> January 2, 1800

He consulted much, pondered much, resolved slowly, resolved surely.

> *Letter from Alexander Hamilton, Concerning the*
> *Public Conduct and Character of John Adams,*
> New York, October 24, 1800

Wealth

The intrinsic wealth of a nation is to be measured not by the abundance of the precious metals contained in it, but by the quantity of the productions of its labor and industry.

> *Report on a National Bank*, Philadelphia, December 13, 1790

If I cannot live *in splendor* in town with a moderate fortune acquired, I can at least live *in comfort* in the country, and I am content to do so.

> To Robert Troup, Albany, New York, April 13, 1795

Wealth and Popularity

It is well known that large property is an object of jealousy in republics and that those who possess it seldom enjoy extensive popularity.

"To the Electors of the State of New York,"
New York, April 7, 1789

Wealth and Poverty

It was certainly true that nothing like an equality of property existed, that an inequality would exist as long as liberty existed, and that it would unavoidably result from that very liberty itself.

Speech at Constitutional Convention,
Philadelphia, June 26, 1787

The West

There is a western country. It *will* be settled. It is in every view best that it should be in great measure settled from abroad rather than at the entire experience [expense] of the Atlantic population. And it is certainly wise by kind treatment to lay hold of the affections of the settlers and attach them from the beginning to the government of the Nation.

To Arthur St. Clair, New York, May 19, 1790

You know my general theory as to our western affairs. I have always held that the unity of our empire and the best interests of

our nation require that we should annex to the UStates all the
territory east of the Mississippia, New Orleans included.

To Charles Cotesworth Pinckney, New York,
December 29, 1802

Whiggism

The spirit of Whiggism is generous, humane, beneficent, and
just. . . . The spirit of Whiggism cherishes legal liberty, holds the
rights of every individual sacred, condemns or punishes no man
without regular trial and conviction of some crime declared [by]
antecedent laws, reprobates equally the punishment of the citizen by arbitrary acts of legislature as by the lawless combinations
of unauthorized individuals.

A Letter from Phocion, New York, January 1-27, 1784

Whigs and Tories

It has been pertinently remarked by a judicious writer that *Caesar*, who *overturned* the republic, was the WHIG, *Cato*, who *died*
for it, the TORY of Rome.

"Catullus No. III," Philadelphia, September 29, 1792

Yards

I like elbow room in a yard.

To Walter Stewart, New York, August 5, 1790

Zeal

It often happens that our zeal is at variance with our understanding.

To William Gordon, West Point, New York,
September 5, 1779

SELECT ANNOTATED BIBLIOGRAPHY

Primary Sources

Cooke, Jacob E., ed. *The Reports of Alexander Hamilton.* New York, 1964. A collection of Hamilton's most important papers on public finance.

Freeman, Joanne B., ed. *Alexander Hamilton: Writings.* New York, 2001. A comprehensive one-volume edition of Hamilton's writings.

Goebel, Julius, Jr., et al., eds. *The Law Practice of Alexander Hamilton: Documents and Commentary.* 5 vols. New York, 1964-81. The definitive edition of Hamilton's legal papers, although more remarkable for its erudite discussion of the law than for the legal documents that Hamilton left behind.

Rossiter, Clinton, ed. *The Federalist Papers.* New York, 1961. Inexpensive edition of the classic commentary on the Constitution, including the 52 essays (out of 85) written by Hamilton.

Syrett, Harold C., et al., eds. *The Papers of Alexander Hamilton.* 27 vols. New York, 1961-87. The best and most comprehensive edition of Hamilton's writings; superbly done and now a model for other projects of this kind.

Secondary Sources

Bower, Aly. *The Rhetoric of Alexander Hamilton.* New York, 1941. An interesting critique of Hamilton's use of the written and spoken word through 1788, although somewhat flawed by factual errors.

Brookhiser, Richard. *Alexander Hamilton: American*. New York, 1999. A short, popular biography that has some good insights.

Cooke, Jacob E. *Alexander Hamilton*. New York, 1982. A psychoanalytical study that emphasizes the effects of Hamilton's childhood on his later life.

Chernow, Ron. *Alexander Hamilton*. New York, 2004. The latest and probably the best study of Hamilton by one of America's most gifted biographers; a dazzling performance that is at once accurate, judicious, and compelling.

Ellis, Joseph J. *Founding Brothers: The Revolutionary Generation*. New York, 2000. An illuminating examination of Hamilton and his generation.

Fleming, Thomas. *The Duel: Alexander Hamilton, Aaron Burr, and the Future of America*. New York, 1999. An account of the famous duel and the events leading up to it.

Freeman, Joanne B. *Affairs of Honor: National Politics in the New Republic*. New Haven, 2001. An innovative analysis of the relationship between dueling and politics in the early republic.

Govan, Thomas P. "Alexander Hamilton and Julius Caesar: A Note on the Use of Historical Evidence," *William and Mary Quarterly*, 3rd Ser., 32 (July 1975): 475-80. Challenges the claim later made by Jefferson that Hamilton considered Caesar the greatest person who ever lived.

Hamilton, Allan McLane. *The Intimate Life of Alexander Hamilton*. New York, 1910. A useful work written by Hamilton's grandson that treats neglected aspects of the great man's personal and family life.

Knott, Stephen F. *Alexander Hamilton and the Persistence of Myth*. Lawrence, KS, 2002. An interesting study of how Hamilton (and to a lesser extent, Jefferson) has been viewed through the ages; concluding chapter seeks to set the record straight on Hamilton.

Lycan, Gilbert L. *Alexander Hamilton and American Foreign Policy: A Design for Greatness*. Norman, OK, 1970. A sympathetic and detailed examination of Hamilton's views on American foreign policy.

McDonald, Forrest. *Alexander Hamilton: A Biography*. New York, 1979. A controversial intellectual biography: brilliant, learned, and very pro-Hamilton.

Miller, John C. *Alexander Hamilton: Portrait in Paradox.* New York, 1959. (The paperback edition is entitled *Alexander Hamilton and the Growth of the New Nation.*) Somewhat dated, but still considered the standard one-volume scholarly biography.

Mitchell, Broadus. *Alexander Hamilton.* 2 vols. New York, 1957-62. The classic life-and-times biography: very detailed and yet eminently readable.

Randall, Willard Sterne. *Alexander Hamilton: A Life.* New York, 2003. A decent popular biography, although the author races through the 1790s (which was Hamilton's most important decade) and pushes his evidence too far.

Rogow, Arnold A. *A Fatal Friendship: Alexander Hamilton and Aaron Burr.* New York, 1998. A balanced, if occasionally speculative, dual biography of the two men who met in the duel that ended Hamilton's life.

Schachner, Nathan. *Alexander Hamilton.* New York, 1946. An older study, still engaging and informative.

Smith, William Ander. "Henry Adams, Alexander Hamilton, and the American People as a 'Great Beast.'" *New England Quarterly* 48 (June 1975): 216-30. Casts doubt on the oft-repeated claim that Hamilton once called the American people "a great beast."

Stourzh, Gerald. *Alexander Hamilton and the Idea of Republican Government.* Stanford, CA, 1970. Analyzes Hamilton's political philosophy and concludes that his vision for an American empire was at its core.

Walling, Karl-Friedrich. *Republican Empire: Alexander Hamilton on War and Free Government.* Lawrence, KS, 1999. A compelling re-interpretation of Hamilton which argues that he was not a militarist.

INDEX

Great Britain, 2, 67–68
Greene, Catherine, 120
Greene, Nathanael, 136

"Hambden," 82
Hamilton, Alexander: affair, 6;
    birth, 1, 13; brother, 14;
    burial, 17; cabinet member,
    5–6; children, 8, 14, 17;
    death, 8, 17; duel, 8;
    education, 2; father, 1, 13, 16;
    financial plan, 4–5; honorary
    degrees, 15; and hurricane, 2,
    13; Inspector General of
    Army, 7, 16; law practice, 6;
    legacy, 8–9; "The Little
    Lion," 3; military campaigns,
    2; military commissions, 2;
    military discharge, 17;
    mother, 1, 13; scouting
    missions, 3; Secretary of
    Treasury, 4–5, 15–16;
    speeches, 2–4; wife, 14;
    writings of, 2–7
Hamilton College, 16
Hamilton, Elizabeth, 33, 41, 43,
    49, 69–70, 90, 109, 114.
    See also Schuyler, Elizabeth
Hamilton, James A., 14, 46
Hamilton Oneida Academy, 16
Hamilton, Philip A., 14, 17, 129
Hamilton, William, 132
happiness, 70
Harison, Richard, 78, 123
Harlem, New York, 8
"H. G." letters, 15; Letter II,
    158; Letter IV, 72, 88; Letter
    XII, 46
Hoffman, Josiah Ogden, 140
honesty, 71
honor, 71
"Horatius No. II," 109

human affairs, 72
human nature, 72–73
hurricane, 2, 73
husband, finding, 54
Hylton v. United States, 6, 147

immigration, 74
impeachment, 74
implied powers, 5, 75
independence, 76
industry and frugality, 76
inheritance, 76
institutions, 77
integrity, 77
interest rates, 77
international blame, 78
international compromise, 78
international law, 78
intolerance, 79
Iredell, James, 6

Jackson, William, 26, 120
Jay, John, 4–5, 26, 28–30, 32,
    99–100, 120, 142, 144
Jay Treaty, 5, 16
jealousy, 79
Jefferson, Thomas, 5, 7–9, 15,
    17, 49, 79–81, 149; and Aaron
    Burr, 7, 17, 81; and James
    Madison, 5, 15, 81;
    presidency, 82
Jeffersonian Republicans, 82
Jews, 83
Johnson, William S., 3
judges, 83
judicial review, 6, 83–84
judicial tyranny, 84
judiciary, federal, 54

Kent, James, 6
King, Rufus, 47, 50, 56, 73, 82,
    121, 124, 126

ABOUT THE EDITORS

Donald R. Hickey holds a Ph.D. from the University of Illinois and is a professor of history at Wayne State College. A specialist in early American history and American military history, Hickey is the author of *The War of 1812: A Forgotten Conflict and Nebraska Moments: Glimpses of Nebraska's Past*. Hickey spent three summers (1988–1990) on the Great Plains Chautauqua circuit portraying Alexander Hamilton. He has performed in more than a dozen states and has been featured on C-Span. Hickey continues to do portrayals of Hamilton, most notably at the annual Toll Fellows Conference sponsored every fall by the Council of State Governments in Lexington, KY.

Connie D. Clark holds an MAE from Wayne State College in Nebraska. A freelance editor and consultant, she has served as editor and publisher of *Senior Life*, a regional magazine geared for senior citizens, and as editor of *Profile*, a national trade publication for community action agencies. Currently, she does freelance editing and is consulting on two Teaching of American History grants for Educational Service Unit #2 in Fremont, Nebraska.